forgotten

TALES

of

ARKANSAS

forgotten TALES of ARKANSAS

Edward L. Underwood &
Karen J. Underwood

THE
History
PRESS

Published by The History Press
Charleston, SC 29403
www.historypress.net

First published 2012

Manufactured in the United States

ISBN 978.1.60949.638.8

Library of Congress CIP data applied for.

To all those who understand Arkansas

Contents

Foreword

I am proud to say that I am a native Arkansan, born and raised in the state's Delta region. Arkansas is a special place, and many people don't "get" that. Edward and Karen Underwood are not those people.

Though not a native of the Natural State (we won't discuss his "Yankee raising"), Ed's love of Arkansas is apparent in his writing. Karen is expected to show her allegiance to Arkansas, since she was raised here. Yet Karen has allowed her love of the state to blossom and grow into devotion, respect and appreciation for Arkansas, its history and its people. Ed simply realized he loved the state and set out to learn everything he could about it. His knowledge of Arkansas exceeds that of most natives. Together, they paint a picture of the true Arkansas—the odd, the amazing, the beautiful and the historic.

I learned a few things about my home state while reading *Forgotten Tales of Arkansas*. As one who has been fascinated by the British monarchy since I was a kid, I was shocked to read that a pearl from Arkansas's famed White River is set in the Royal Crown of England. I had no idea that baby physician extraordinaire Dr. Benjamin Spock once called Rogers, Arkansas, home.

As a travel writer for Arkansas Parks and Tourism, the best part of my job is traveling this beautiful state and learning more about the history and culture of the place I happily call home. If you've never visited the Natural State, I suggest you correct that situation immediately.

Kim Williams
Arkansas Travel Writer
www.visitmyarkansas.com

PREFACE

I grew up in a Yankee family. There, I said it. Prior to the year of our lord 1976, my only experience with America's Natural State was an incident that occurred when I was very young. My family was on a road trip during vacation and, while passing through Arkansas, had to pull over and take a picture in front of a sign identifying a city we were about to enter. So taken were we northerners with the name of this place that we put the vintage Polaroid camera to work in order to prove its existence to our friends back home. The name of this town called forth nearly endless peals of laughter and mirth. There, on the official state-approved road sign, were the bright letters spelling out "Bald Knob."

Little did we realize that Bald Knob is a rather reasonable name for an Arkansas town. Over the next few years, the karma fairies were hard at work engineering a diabolical scheme in which we would return to this land of euphonious appellations. In 1976, we become Arkansans.

Arkansas is a place of colorful extremes. The scenery goes from nature to neon and from universities to roadside shopping attractions like this. *Photo by Heather Stanley.*

We then learned many startling facts and figures about our new home state, including names of towns that make "Bald Knob" sound majestic and stately.

Here are just a few of our favorite names of actual Arkansas cities: Goobertown, Weiner, Fannie, Bloomer, Hooker, Blue Ball, Toad Suck, Nob Hill, Beaver, Mount Ida, Mount Holly, Yellville, Ola, Biggers, Smackover, Turkey Scratch, Possum Grape, Oil Trough, Hope, Fifty, Magazine, Rector, Hog Wallow, Hog Jaw, Ash Flat, Greasy

Corner, Gassville, Flippin, Salem, Natural Steps, Stinking Bay, Pickles Gap, Birds Town, Pottsville, Egypt, Sulphur Springs and Hicksville.

So I wish to thank my family for making me part of the Arkansas experience. It has made me wiser, stronger and far more likely to believe that any ridiculous thing might, in fact, be true.

Edward L. Underwood

Even though I was born in the sunny state of California, both sides of my family are generational Arkansans. My father's family is from the tiny little community of Manson, near Walnut Ridge. My mother's family came from the town of Bay. Both areas are part of the Delta region of our state. The Delta is characterized by its low-lying flood zones, challenging roads and nearly endless rice, soybean and cotton fields.

It is also characterized by the people. In addition to my family and my husband, I have met some of the most wonderful, caring, talented, faithful and determined people here. And a few cantankerous fools, too. The Delta also infuses a mentality into its people. The dependence on the land has made them well acquainted with sorrow and disappointment.

Human beings have no choice when it comes to the hardship and suffering we experience in life. But where we do have a choice is our response. We can become bitter or better. Like the rose or like the thorn, we can blossom or we can become harsh and wound others when they touch us. I have observed both responses during my time in Arkansas.

In an effort to be simple and straightforward, there is no time for the "frills" in life. Necessity and the importance of religion sccm to choke out the very things that actually give life its beauty and meaning.

But I see glimmers of hope everywhere. Arkansas is a strange alchemy of the truly beautiful and the truly bizarre. The future depends on each individual and the decisions made moment to moment. Each day is a new opportunity to decide.

Karen Underwood

We want to say thank you to the librarians, curators and educators who assisted our search for ever more obscure information. Special thanks to Marti Allen at the Arkansas State University Museum and Brandi Hodges at the Craighead County Public Library for help and access above and beyond all rational justification! A big thank you goes to our good friend Kim Williams for contributing the foreword to this book. No one works harder to promote the state of Arkansas than she.

We must acknowledge the support and encouragement of our creative friends and partners, including Kenton

Now who wouldn't stop for a free map and stock up on fireworks and ammo from a store with a grizzly bear? It's all part of the Bizarrkansas experience. *Photo by Heather Stanley.*

Knepper, Paul Prater, Ralph Forbis, Jackie Scott and Wylie Marvin. The same goes for our friends at Arkansas State University: Mark Smith, Marti Allen, Richard Carvell and Libby James. And much thanks and love to our son, Kevin, who keeps the band together, and daughter, Heather, and her husband, Jonathan Stanley, for encouragement and terrific pictures and artwork. And finally, thanks to The History Press for reminding America about Arkansas through this quirky tome of forgotten tales.

1

WELCOME TO BIZARRKANSAS

Step right up ladies and gentlemen, boys and girls. Don't be afraid to gaze wide eyed at the wonders of a state that sports nature and neon, celebrated cities and tiny towns and acres and acres of variegated vegetation as diverse as its own cultural past.

A place filled to overflowing with colorful heroes and villains. A place where the future and the past remain uneasy acquaintances, while old-tyme faith, long-standing vices and bare-knuckle politics are fast friends.

A culture built on equal parts folklore and facts, stories and statistics. Where ghosts still haunt with unbridled vigor and the tales of superstitious old-timers are faithfully retold to shape a new generation's worldview.

A land possessed of unspeakable natural beauty and nearly boundless natural resources, a land that is a representative snapshot of the American journey. The bravery, independence and fierce determination that

Arkansas is called the Natural State for good reason—like these cascading waterfalls at Blanchard Springs. *Photo by Heather Stanley.*

shaped our nation is seen in microcosm in this wild, wooly, wonderful place that is still very much one of America's frontier states.

As you draw closer to the spectacle that we call "Bizarrkansas," you will see contrasts around every turn! There will be oddities and antiquities. Universities next to miles of untouched forest, cities planted in the middle of rice fields. And you can bet that each one of these phenomena has enough history and tall tales attached to it to fill an entire afternoon.

Keep a sharp eye as you pass through America's Natural State or you might miss something amazing or, at the very least, unusual. If you enter the state from the northwest, you might pass through Eureka Springs, a fabled location for magical healing water, ghosts and wild-eyed crusaders. A place currently inhabited by artists, writers, craftsmen of all kinds and a million or so tourists annually. And yes, there are still ghosts and wild-eyed crusaders.

Cross our border at the southwest corner and you can have your picture taken on Stateline Avenue in Texarkana,

Breathtaking natural beauty can be seen all over the state. *Photo by Heather Stanley.*

with one foot in Texas and the other in Arkansas. Please watch for oncoming traffic.

Our western border at Oklahoma includes the city of Fort Smith—a city founded in 1817 as a military outpost dedicated to helping settle the Wild West. Its nickname is "hell on the border," while its motto is "Life's worth living." Both phrases ring true.

At the northeast corner is Jonesboro, home of Arkansas State University; Riceland Foods, Inc.; pole vault champion Earl Bell; novelist John Grisham; and comedian Roger Bumpass, best known as the voice of Squidward Tentacles on *Spongebob Squarepants*.

So armed with the knowledge that our path will be filled with contrasts, contradictions and cold hard facts that may seem hard to believe, we welcome you to our celebration of the bizarre and beautiful, the absurd and the amazing, the impossible and the highly unlikely buried within these *Forgotten Tales of Arkansas*.

2

A Collection of Arcane Arkan-Knowledge

Before we wade into the deep, deep waters of the bizarre and forgotten realms of Arkansas history, let us begin with a crash course in simple yet unbelievable facts about America's Natural State. Here to begin our journey is a compilation of true things you should know. Let's begin with the most basic anomaly about Arkansas: the very word "Arkansas" itself.

Arkansas. I know what you're thinking. You pronounce Arkansas like "Ark and Saw." But somewhere deep inside you, the years of book learnin', schoolin' and worldly travel lead you to the inescapable, clear conclusion that the word "Arkansas" should, in fact, be pronounced "Ar-Kansas." So, Arkansas, what's up with that? In what will soon become a familiar theme in the course of our study, we find that history and folklore have collided to provide us with a colorful answer.

It seems that the name Arkansas comes from the same root word for the name of the state of Kansas. This word came from the names of American Indian tribes that, when mixed with a French pronunciation and vocal styling, emphasize the "aw"-sounding ending instead of that suggested by the spelling ("sus").

In 1881, two Arkansas senators began to dispute and fight with each other over the correct way to say the state's name. It seems that up to this point in history, as many people were saying "Ar-Kansas" as "Ark and Saw." After much lobbying and argument, the state legislature made the pronunciation of "Ark and Saw" official. This, then, was the first official blow for counterintuitive decision-making by the state's leadership.

And in 2007, the legislature passed the official pronouncement that the possessive form of the state was to be rendered as "Arkansas's." State government and education have also adopted this rule of grammar. So, now you know.

THE STATE FLAG

Miss Willie Hocker of Wabbasseka created the Arkansas state flag in the year 1913, when the battleship called the USS *Arkansas* was commissioned. A chapter of the Daughters of the American Revolution discovered that the state had no official flag to fly on the deck of the ship, so it held a contest to find an appropriate design.

The original design of the flag is very close to that of the current flag, with a couple notable exceptions. The first flag was a diamond in white with three blue stars straight across the diamond. The diamond shape was taken from the fact that Arkansas was the only state in America that was actively mining diamonds.

The three stars represented three aspects of state history. First, they represented the fact that Arkansas had been part of three countries: the United States, France and Spain. Second, the Louisiana Purchase made Arkansas part of the United States in 1803. And finally, Arkansas was the third state created out of the Louisiana Purchase. A border of twenty-five stars recalled that Arkansas was the twenty-fifth state of the Union.

But alas, before this fetching work of art and symbolism was to be accepted by the state legislature, it was requested that the flag receive a symbol to represent the Confederacy.

Now, let us not forget that the whole thing looks shockingly similar to the actual Confederate flag in the first place. It seems you just can't get too much Confederate worked into your identity in Arkansas. And so, a single star was added above the name of the state.

It was, however, noted that the single star for the Confederacy made the whole thing look ironically off center. That issue was settled by deciding to offset to the right one of three original stars below the state's name. So this nod to the Confederacy, insisted on in 1913, resulted in a state flag that obviously "leans to the right." Today, there are a few variations on the state flag with more symmetrical spacing of its symbolic stars.

FORGOTTEN FACTS FROM THE NATURAL STATE

- Pugh's Mill in North Little Rock was used in the opening sequence of *Gone With the Wind*.
- Arkansas bears the distinction of being the only state in the Union that outlawed the teaching of evolution by popular vote. You need never fear that anything is evolving here.
- Arkansas's state motto is *Regnant populous*, meaning, "Let the people rule."
- A gallows was built in Fort Smith that could hang twelve men at the same time. Judge Isaac Parker hanged no fewer than seventy-nine criminals between the years 1875 and 1896.
- Baby care and child development guru Dr. Benjamin Spock lived near Rogers, Arkansas.
- A National Lum and Abner Society has a convention on the Saturday after Father's Day every year in Mena, Arkansas. Lum and Abner helped make Arkansas famous. They also helped create the stereotypes that the state has never been able to escape.
- Sugar Loaf Mountain, an island in Greer's Ferry Lake, can only be accessed by boat.

Inside Blanchard Springs Cavern. *Photo by Heather Stanley.*

- Arkansas has an annual rainfall of forty-nine inches.
- Cosmic Cavern in Berryville has the world's largest underground bridge and a rock formation that many say looks like Santa Claus.
- Arkansas used to be known as the "Bear State" due to its enormous population of bears. Other slogans that were eventually cast off include the "Bowie State" and the "Toothpick State" (both of which were references to the Bowie knife), the "Razorback State," the "Hotwater State," the "Wonder State" and the "Land of Opportunity." The Land of Opportunity name was adopted in 1947 and remained official for thirty-eight

years. Arkansas is currently known as the "Natural State." This is the most logical nickname, as Arkansas does have nearly limitless amounts of nature.

- Arkansas has also collected a number of nicknames/slogans that are either a) humorous or b) satirical and vicious. These include a number of things that can easily be bought on T-shirts and bumper stickers, including "Arkansas—Where Your Daddy Is Your Uncle," "Literassy Ain't Everything," "Arkansas Safe Sex: We Mark the Sheep that Kick" and "We Pluck a Mean Chicken."

The War Eagle Mill in Rogers, Arkansas, is one of the only operating natural water-powered gristmills in the country. It dates back to pre–Civil War days. Today, it is a tourist attraction that offers visitors a look at the milling process, two floors of gift shops and a third-floor loft café. *Photo by Dean Mundungis.*

War Eagle also offers visitor an authentic Arkansas outhouse experience. *Photo by Dean Mundungis.*

- Arkansas's history with bears and diamonds led to the state's award-winning brewery being called Diamond Bear Beer, located outside Little Rock. The brewery has become very successful; it won multiple awards for its flavor blends and is a popular tourist spot.
- *Ripley's Believe It Or Not!* newspaper column documented the story of Mady Armstrong, who in 1936 built an actual house in Searcy using thirteen thousand dimes saved from odd jobs over ten years.
- Burt Reynolds's TV sitcom *Evening Shade* was based on the town of Evening Shade, and the title was (so they say) suggested by then first lady Hillary Clinton.

- The Ozark Folk Center in Mountain View is known as the Folk Music Capital of the World. The center hosts an impressive variety of indigenous musicians on a stage decorated to look like an old-time back porch.

A replica of an old-time Arkansas schoolhouse. This and other historic re-creations take place at the Ozark Mountain Folk Center in Mountain View, Arkansas. *Photo by Heather Stanley.*

- The Quindell, a cross between a red delicious and an old-fashioned Winesap apple, is a patented Arkansas fruit.
- Arkansas apples won over two hundred medals and took all top awards at the St. Louis World's Fair in 1904.
- From 1864 through 1865, Arkansas had two state governments. One was Confederate and the other Union. They both operated at once without acknowledging each other.
- *Arkansas* is the Indian term for the "downstream people."
- A house on Cantrell Street in Little Rock once sported over 1.5 million red Christmas lights.
- Jonesboro is home to the world's largest commercial rice mill, operated by Riceland Foods.
- King Vidor made the first movie shot in Arkansas. It was called *Hallelujah* and was produced and shot in 1929. The film was one of the first all-black movies backed by a major Hollywood studio. It was a musical about faith and the forbidden. It was such a risky venture that the studio asked Vidor to stake his own salary in the production cost. In the end, the film earned an Oscar nomination and is now considered a neglected American classic.
- Concert Vineyards in Lakeview grows over two hundred varieties of grapes, including the Cynthiana, one of Arkansas's native grapes.
- It is estimated that there are nearly four thousand alligators in the state. A bit later, we will introduce you to Big Arky, one of the most famous gators from Arkansas.

- *Li'l Abner* took place in the fictional town of Dogpatch. An actual amusement park was created as Dogpatch, USA, near the real town of Harrison. We will tell you all about this experiment in absurdity in a later chapter.
- Ray Suggett, resident of West Fork, invented the now familiar fake vomit, melted ice cream and dismembered finger novelties. Can we ever thank him enough for the memories?
- The Bible Museum in Eureka Springs holds more than seven thousand Bibles and other obscure manuscripts in 625 languages.
- The effort to put the phrase "In God We Trust" on U.S. money was led by Matt Rothert from Camden, Arkansas, back in 1955.

Eureka Springs, Arkansas, is an artists' colony with art hiding around every corner. Here is a giant mural that depicts the story of the town's origin on the side of a downtown building. *Photo by Heather Stanley.*

- Moon rocks were stored in Hot Springs' spring water while NASA was searching for signs of life on them. Arkansas has always been the home of natural spring water considered to have mystical properties.
- Heber Springs' feline fisher Boots has an actual fishing license from the Arkansas Game and Fish Commission. Her biggest catch is reported to have been twelve inches long.
- Alan Ladd, the popular actor who will be forever famous for his role in the classic western movie *Shane*, was born in Hot Springs on September 13, 1913.
- During a freakish hailstorm in 1973, completely frozen ducks fell to the ground in Stuttgart. A number of such bizarre atmospheric episodes have occurred in Arkansas, including New Year's Day and the following days of 2011, when over 100,000 fish and five thousand blackbirds washed ashore and fell from the sky dead over the small town of BeBee.
- The town of Hector was named after President Cleveland's pet bulldog.
- Arkansas continues to be one of the top five states for retirement. A low cost of living continues to make the state attractive to retirees.
- President Bill Clinton was born in the city of Hope, as William Jefferson Blythe IV, on August 19, 1946. Mr. Clinton was (oddly enough) the forty-second governor of Arkansas and the forty-second president of the United States. The Clintons' cat Socks was the twelfth

Karen directs your attention to the giant roadside raven at Ravenden Springs. *Photo by Heather Stanley.*

cat in the White House. Socks had a sister living in Little Rock during his tenure as "First Pet."

- One of the nation's most successful retailers is Dillard's, with over 225 locations. Its head office is in Little Rock.
- Arkansas is the number one rice-producing state in America. The rice fields themselves keep Arkansas a top mosquito-producing state as well.
- Maybelline Incorporated in Little Rock is the largest producer of domestic cosmetic products.

In many states, the giant raven would simply be a mascot, but in Arkansas, it will have a biblical connection to explain its existence. *Photo by Heather Stanley.*

- Aromatic International was created by Jonesboro native Patti Upton. Her initials are—ironically—P.U.
- A pearl from Arkansas's White River resides in the Royal Crown of England.

3

PRAISE THE LORD
AND PASS THE AMMO

Arkansas is in the southern part of the United States known as the Bible Belt. Arguably, it may be the buckle on the Bible Belt that holds up the trousers of righteousness over the legs of faith that walk to church. And it won't be a long walk. Statistically, there are fifteen churches for every 10,000 persons. Now, let's break that down to an eye-opening cryptic Bible Belt statistic: one church for every 666 people. The number 666 is the biblical number of the beast.

Anywhere else, that statistic might be thought of as an interesting and humorous coincidence. But in Arkansas, such things are taken very seriously. In fact, it might be more than fair to say that no other force has more sway over the minds and cultural lives of Arkansas citizens. I would go so far as to say that though it is rarely viewed in such terms, religion is Arkansas's major industry and most robust employer.

This beautiful statue adorns the entryway to St. Elizabeth's Cathedral in Eureka Springs. *Photo by Heather Stanley.*

Big churches, mega churches, simple churches and tiny, tiny churches, along with the parachurch operations that support them and the bookstores and suppliers that support the industry, are present in every corner of even the smallest Arkansas town.

The first recorded Christian worship service is believed to have been conducted by Roman Catholic priests who accompanied the expedition of Hernando de Soto. The event took place in 1541 near what is now known as Parkin, Arkansas, in Cross County.

Arkansas's religious makeup at the time of this writing is tallied the following way: Christians make up 86 percent of the population. Of those, 78 percent are Protestants.

The denominations break down as follows:

Baptist: 39 percent
Methodist: 9 percent
Pentecostal: 6 percent
Church of Christ: 6 percent
Assemblies of God: 3 percent
Other Protestants: 15 percent

Non-Protestant denominations include:

Roman Catholic: 7 percent
Orthodox: less than 1 percent
Mormon/LDS: less than 1 percent
Other Christian groups: less than 1 percent

More art from inside St. Elizabeth's. *Photo by Heather Stanley.*

Other religions account for less than 1 percent. (At least, that's what the survey answers reported.) Non-religious beliefs account for 14 percent. (These folks are so getting a Wednesday night visitation!) And the Jewish faith is .01 percent.

Given the fact that Arkansas began as a sea of non-Christian ruffians, the current social climate is a tribute to the dedication and perseverance of its true believers—and the peer pressure they command.

STAVE A FERVOR, PART I

With religion playing such a key role in Arkansas life and culture, you might imagine that we have had our fair share of memorable, and perhaps forgotten, religiously driven characters. You would be right! To suggest that some of these figures fanned the flames of the faithful, fervent flocks to the point of insanity would be an understatement.

Enjoy, if you will, two tales of straight-out crazy for God. I'll remind you now that both of these twisted adventures are true. And that living, breathing human beings equipped with the power of reason, speech and thought were party to all that happened. I remind you of that now because halfway through this account you are going to question it.

My Arkansas hometown—the kindly city of Jonesboro—was given the nickname the "city of churches." The first two churches to incorporate and establish themselves were First Baptist Church and First United Methodist Church.

At this time, Jonesboro has an official population of 66,000 and over 225 churches. That's a church for every 290 persons in town. Nearly 100 of those churches are of the Baptist denominational persuasion.

Most everyone here has, by design, forgotten that the little town of Jonesboro found itself on the front page of the *New York Times* for a religious holy war, a fundamentalist jihad of the Christian sort, that would actually result in violence against elected officials, gun battles in the streets, murder, slander and the National Guard occupying the town under martial law.

And most ironic of all, Jonesboro's holy war would make the cover of the *New York Times* on September 11. The September 11, 1931 front-page story reads, "Church Fight Leads to Use of Troops." So settle back and prepare yourself for a tale of religious conviction, political fervor and violence in the name of God.

Let me also point out that the good people who work, worship and serve in the current incarnations of these churches had nothing to do with the insanity that gripped the town during the "great church war."

When the sun came up on June 29, 1930, no one suspected just how profoundly the preacher at the tent revival organized by the First Baptist Church and the Jonesboro Bible College would shake the town with his fiery blood-bought, devil-fought Gospel!

The preacher's name was Joe Jeffers. Mr. Jeffers's prior occupation was that of comedian and actor. He had only recently become a licensed and ordained Baptist evangelist. No one was sure where he came from, but they did know that he was shot at twice that spring in St. Louis for speaking out against gambling. During a card game.

He seemed to be a man who feared only God. Mr. Jeffers was described as being devastatingly well spoken, charming, funny and endlessly captivating.

First Baptist Church stands proudly on Main Street, and the tent for the crusade was erected just off the church grounds. Mr. Jeffers electrified the crowds, and attendance grew past everything the organizers had hoped and prayed for. Night after night, capacity crowds crammed in and around the tent. It seemed clear to the church leaders that God had sent this special man to do very special work in a special way in the town. They were filled with excitement over the idea that Jonesboro would never again be spiritually the same.

Jeffers was such a hit that the crusade was extended through the month of July. So thrilled was the leadership of the church and Bible school that in August, when First Baptist's pastor A.W. Reaves resigned, the congregation rushed to offer the electrifying Mr. Jeffers the pastorate.

Expectations were high among the church members and leadership about just how far this work of God might reach through the astounding and anointed Mr. Jeffers. It was at this precise moment that things took a turn for the worse. It turned out that some of the church members felt they had been left out of the decision-making process. They opposed the decision to offer Jeffers the pastorate and rounded up enough of their own supporters within the congregation to force a vote on the issue. Hard feelings started to take root as the protesting Protestants reversed the leadership's decision. They informed Mr. Jeffers that his services would not be required, and they offered the pastor position to a man named Dow Heard. Joe Jeffers made an angry, but sadly temporary, departure from town.

First Baptist's new pastor was a thirty-five-year-old, well-schooled, redheaded preacher named Dow Heard, whom *Time* magazine described as "lantern jawed." Now here in the South, there is an expression that is used when you realize someone is headed for trouble or in a situation way over his or her head. That expression is: "Bless their heart." And here we must say that, bless his heart, Mr. Heard likely thought his big challenge leading the church would be an inevitable building program. Truly, here was a man who did not and could not have possibly seen the misery coming his way. Before the Jeffers affair was over, he and his family would be publicly ridiculed, accused of personal indiscretions and repeatedly said to be misleading God's elect and obstructing justice in the city.

Mr. Jeffers sent forth the news that he was starting a standing revival meeting ministry in Jonesboro. This created an immediate buzz in town. Everyone who had seen and heard him before was making plans to attend his triumphant return. And those who had only heard the stories of his first crusade were now aquiver with anticipation.

The Jeffers revival tent was pitched less than a quarter mile from First Baptist Church. His first series of messages were sensational, dire warnings that the second coming would take place in May 1932. To be ready and to be counted as a real believer, one must receive the truest of truths and follow the narrowest of narrow ways—both of which Jeffers claimed to represent in contrast to the compromised messages of certain other ministries across the street. These messages were not the same old tired church sermons. These messages were fiery and juicy! And announcing the date of the second coming was just the beginning.

Jeffers next electrified the growing crowds with tales of immorality involving Pastor Heard and Mayor Herbert Bosler. The Svengali-like evangelist had the crowd in the palm of his sweaty hand with these accusations, stories and sensational rumors. Let me put the size of his crowds in perspective for you. In 1931, the population of Jonesboro was just over ten thousand. The attendance at his meetings each night was reported as being as high as seven thousand people.

It was a hot time in the old town when a fistfight broke out between supporters of Heard and supporters of Jeffers. As the two sides rolled to the ground in combat, others joined in, and soon it was a free-for-all. Fists were abandoned for boards, shovels, pitchforks and, in just a few minutes, guns. Yes, it seemed a good portion of the saints wanted to kill one another. Eventually, order was restored, and one of Jeffers's supporters was arrested and charged with assault as the aggressor in the brawl.

The next morning, Jeffers led a band of some five hundred followers to the steps of the courthouse. As the much-maligned mayor arrived, Jeffers requested permission to lead a prayer before the proceedings began. Surrounded by the frothing flock of the faithful, the mayor conceded and offered Mr. Jeffers four minutes for prayer.

Taking his place at the top of the courthouse stairs, Jeffers went into his most theatrical mode and began to implore God Almighty that justice would come to Jonesboro. He asked that God purify Jonesboro from its corrupted political bosses and its misguided, deceived spiritual leaders.

His five minutes turned into fifteen. Fifteen moved on toward thirty minutes as his accusing, insulting "prayer" droned on and on. Now becoming aware that he had been played to look weak in front of the masses, the mayor asked the chief of police to tell Mr. Jeffers to stop and stand down.

This request was met with rejection and hostility from Jeffers and the crowd. He continues to hurl his words at the sky like weapons of mass destruction. The mayor now insisted that the police remove him so they could enter the courthouse and conduct business. Upon the first officer's taking hold of the overbearing orator, Jeffers cried out, "May God strike the mayor dead!" Immediately after that, punches and blows began to fall on any and all city officials within striking distance.

The mayor, chief of police and their officers pushed their way through and into the courthouse, where they locked the door behind them. Mayor Bosler sent a fevered telegram to the governor asking for intervention in the form of troops. His message plainly stated that "thousands of lives are in danger; declare martial law or machine gun down one thousand church members." The mayor and governor determined that the local police were of no use in the conflict as they were also taking sides in the holy war.

The ROTC from Jonesboro and Blytheville managed to round up and deliver seventy-five soldiers. The governor's secretary arrived in Jonesboro with 150 more troops.

The soldiers were stationed around all of the downtown area intersections with firearms ready and bayonets in place. Vehicles with machine guns took up strategic posts around the church, the courthouse and the revival tent grounds. An airplane landed in Jonesboro carrying a load of tear gas bombs for emergency crowd control.

Now, during this time the meeting carried on under special curfew agreements. These stipulations and the presence of the troops did not dampen Jeffers's rhetoric at all. At this point, he began to single out Catholics for ridicule in his services. He dressed in a burlesque of priest's robes and hired a local boy to play an altar boy in his mockery of Catholic Church rituals.

One night, the boy was struck by a car about a block away from the revival and was taken to St. Bernard's Hospital. It is, of course, a Catholic hospital. Once Jeffers was informed of the situation, he led a throng of worshippers down the street to the hospital. Along the way, he cast doubt on how well the Catholics would care for this faithful Protestant boy.

Storming through the front doors and into the lobby, Jeffers demanded to know the status of the boy. He was told by one of the sisters that the young man's condition was quite serious but that they were doing all they could for him. This brought a diatribe of denominational snobbery down on the poor sister's head as the crowd "Amened" and "Hallelujahed" along. Mr. Jeffers demanded to be taken to the boy, where he promised he would heal him and lead him out of the hospital. At roughly that precise moment, another sister came forward and whispered in the ear of the first. The news was given that the boy had died. Jeffers made this incident the centerpiece of his intolerant rants for the next days and weeks.

Through the middle of September, National Guard troops from all over the state were sent in and positioned through the town to keep order. Most of them were put near Jeffers's revival tent. A first attempt to withdraw the soldiers proved only that tempers were still too hot. Violence broke out again but was quickly squelched. Finally, the troops were removed, and it seemed the quiet little town had returned to normal.

Two days after the soldiers were withdrawn, a tear gas bomb was set off outside the revival tent. Soon after that, all identified supporters of Joe Jeffers were expelled from First Baptist Church. And then, on October 25, the revival tent was burned to the ground during the wee hours of the morning. Never one to give up, Mr. Jeffers built the Jonesboro Baptist Church at the corner of Matthews and Cobb Streets. Take that, First Baptist!

Jeffers decided to leave the church and brought in a man named Dale Crowley to serve as pastor. Leaving the work in the hands of this new leader eased tensions in the town considerably. Things seemed to be returning to normal at last. That is, until the silver-tongued devil himself decided to return.

Less than one year after his departure, Mr. Jeffers returned and demanded that Crowley relinquish control of the church back to him. This new wrinkle created a rift within the church that was formed out of the rift with First Baptist Church.

So the two men of God did the only loving thing: they competed for control of the majority of the church's members by holding services at the same time. The two men railed at each other by sermonizing about theology, leadership and morality in an effort to win the allegiance of the people. On August 14, 1933, the church struggle erupted in a fistfight that spilled out into the streets until shotguns were loaded and aimed on both sides.

Perhaps thinking they would avoid bloodshed, the two leaders agreed to let the courts decide the fate of the church. On October 9, the courts ruled in favor of Mr. Crowley's keeping leadership of the church. You might be tempted to think that settled the issue once and for all. You would be wrong about that. We are talking about people with real convictions, which in this case could mean strong personal beliefs as well as criminal records. Read on, oh seeker of truth and light.

When Mr. Crowley headed back to take his court-appointed place as leader of the church, he was shot at by a man named J.W. McMurdo. McMurdo was hired by Jeffers as a janitor, but his personal skill set centered more on guns than brooms. Crowley escaped the assault, but his bodyguard, L.H. Kayre, was wounded. Before the exchange was over, McMurdo was shot three times and died from the wounds. Joe Crowley found himself arrested, but he claimed his actions were strictly in self-defense.

Now, you might think that the town, its leaders and officials had grown tired of Jeffers and Crowley and the nonstop trouble they had caused. In that, you would be right. On October 17, an unknown individual stuck the barrel of a machine gun into Crowley's jail cell. Amazingly, despite the rain of bullets, sharp shards of cement and brick, Crowley was not killed.

Law enforcement officials sent the bruised and bandaged Crowley out of Jonesboro to the town of Piggott for his trial. He was acquitted of the murder charge and released.

Meanwhile, the always-resilient Reverend Jeffers hid out in Miami and renounced his titles and ties to the Baptist denomination. He did this in order to become the leader of the Pyramid Power Yahweh group in Missouri. He went from comedian and actor to evangelist to pastor to church planter to gunfighter to self-proclaimed prophet! Mr. Jeffers led his pyramid flock for many years, building attendance with his tales of fighting evil in Jonesboro.

Soon, Heard and Crowley both left Jonesboro as well. To this day, there are bitter memories of the Jonesboro church wars. Very few locals have ever spoken out on the episode, and members of the churches, of course, have hoped for decades that the story would fade away forever. History

Found on the floor of a chapel in northwest Arkansas. The quieter, more meditative side of religious expression is less popular than more vocal approaches in the South. *Photo by Heather Stanley.*

teaches us that what reads like unthinkable insanity today might well have seemed logical, warranted and, dare we say, even righteous in a heated moment of misguided devotion.

The Jonesboro Church War of 1931 is a truly forgotten bit of Arkansas's history. Let us hope that the lessons it will teach to future generations of zealous followers will not be forgotten.

Stave a Fervor, Part II: Remember the Alamo

There once was a man who became famous as an evangelist, preacher and crusader. He and his wife hosted television shows and radio programs, recorded songs, wrote books and tracts and traveled all over the world spreading their version of the good news.

Sadly, at the height of this man's fame and power, his wife died of cancer. This was particularly sad, as this man went on to claim that God told him his wife would be resurrected from the dead. He kept her body on display at his ministry headquarters in Dyer, Arkansas, and asked his followers to keep praying for her to reanimate and rise. Which they did. But she didn't.

Two years after her death, the man married another woman and tried to convince her to have cosmetic surgery to make her look identical to his deceased and, as yet, unresurrected spouse. Was he planning a switcheroo that would look like a miracle to his faithful, fervent flock? She refused the surgery and divorced this maniacal man of the cloth. But the followers still believed.

Ten years later, when federal agents headed out to raid his ministry compound, he told his followers to take his wife's body and run away with it. They did. After a three-year court battle and a total of sixteen years after her death, the woman's body was returned to her family and given a proper burial.

That man's name was Tony Alamo. Surely, you remember the Alamo? Well, maybe not, as his real name was Bernie

Hoffman. His wife's name was Susan Alamo. Well, actually, it was Edith Horn.

The twisted tale of how these two came to embody the worst stereotypes of the "raging righteous" would require an entire book of its own! In the interest of time and sanity, we shall merely give you the highlights and leave further research up to you. Just a word of caution if you do undertake further study: Mr. Hoffman's early life is almost impossible to unwind from a network of self-aggrandizing lies and exaggerations created to make his Christian testimony all the more astounding to the crowds.

Bernie was born in Joplin, Missouri, in the year 1934. He says his father was a Romanian immigrant who taught Rudolph Valentino to dance. In his teen years, Bernie claims to have taken the stage name of Marcus Abad for the purpose of a successful career as a lounge crooner in Hollywood. He claims to have recorded a hit single called "Little Yankee Girl" before owning a private health club and moving on to manage big-name music acts, including The Beatles, the Rolling Stones and The Doors. There is, however, no proof of any of this.

As fate would have it, an Arkansas native named Edith Horn was also trying to make it in Hollywood at the same time. Twice divorced and traveling with a young daughter, Edith had no success breaking into the movies but found quite a bit of success running a scam on evangelical churches.

Edith would tell the churches that she was an overseas missionary trying to raise money to continue the good work.

The churches responded with cash, and soon this scam became Edith's settled career path. Meanwhile, Bernie was walking out of jail after serving time on a weapons charge when the two met, and the rest, as they say, is history. Well, history and a long police record.

The two married and were converted to Christianity after a personal visit from Jesus during a Beverly Hills investment meeting. The pair then became the newly born-again Tony and Susan Alamo. They launched into street-level ministry with unbridled passion and soon built up the organization that came to be known as the Tony Alamo Christian Ministries.

The organization bought buildings to house the homeless, feed the poor, rehabilitate drug addicts and give shelter to society's most forsaken members. The Alamos grew a mighty financial empire out of all this helping and serving.

Outsiders did not know that while the financial ledgers of the ministry were running over with donation monies, those in the service centers were scrounging for food out of dumpsters, and residents were warned not to flush the toilets more than three times a day so as not to waste "God's resources."

In 1975, the Alamos bought land in Dyer, Arkansas, and opened a church and the first of several properties. Tony and Susan also started the first of twenty-nine (or more!) businesses in and around the little town. In each of these businesses ranging from restaurants to western-wear stores, the employees were chosen from those receiving "ministry" and therefore received little or often no pay for their employment.

By 1976, the federal government was on to the Alamos for wage and hiring fraud, along with an ever-growing list of crimes and scams dating back to the beginning of their ministry. Soon the government and its lawyers had Tony and Susan in their sights.

Now, to anyone else, this may have meant that the jig was up. But to the Alamos, and more amazingly, to those who continued to believe and trust them, it meant that Brother Alamo's messages were in fact prophetic and inspired. You see, the cornerstone of the message the Alamos championed was the idea that the government, the Vatican, the United Nations and the media were under Satan's control and would try to wipe out anyone who dared expose this truth.

So the fact that Satan's minions had come swooping down on the prophet and his wife was sweet, sweet vindication that he was telling the truth. It's a mind-warping, pretzel logic that is fairly common in extremist circles of all kinds.

Susan, as we mentioned back at the start, died in 1982. From the mid-1980s on, Tony was always in a court and/or prison situation. During the next two decades, he found time to marry another woman. It was disclosed that this third marriage should have been counted as his sixth. He was married numerous times, and to this day, no one is sure how many times he was married under how many names.

Alamo also began marrying "child brides" from the ministry compound families. This brought charges of child abuse and molestation down upon him. Tony and his lawyers fought for years and years until finally, in 2009, he was found guilty on nine counts of transporting minors over state lines for the purpose of sex. He is currently serving out a 175-year prison sentence.

The hard-to-believe part is that Tony Alamo can still be heard preaching his fearful conspiracies on a dozen or more Arkansas radio stations, and his books and tracts are still in print and distributed by the remaining faithful believers he created.

4

NOAH LOOKED OUT OF THE
ARK AND SAW

So much does Arkansas love its Bible lore that on many
occasions it has attempted to re-create biblical events
for itself. Specifically, universal flooding. The natural
conditions of the state, particularly the northeastern Delta
region, are perfect for flooding. In fact, large sections of the
state remained under water until one hundred years ago or
so. Some travel websites remind adventurers that you can
easily find shark teeth and other marine fossils and relics in
the fertile, moist ground of Arkansas.

Now known as the Great Arkansas Flood of 1927, it was
the greatest flood event in North American history and
the fourth-greatest flood in recorded world history (Noah's
flood being a notable exception).

Thirty-six counties were affected, with water smothering
over 13 percent of the state's land area. The cause of the
flood is, of course, most curious. It seems that heavy rains
in the central basin area of the Mississippi River over the

Flooding was so familiar to the northeast and Delta regions of Arkansas that wealthy folks invested in watertight lead coffins. The weight would help prevent the coffins from floating up to the surface, and the moveable face windows could identify bodies if they were displaced. This was found in the Arkansas State University Museum collection. *Photo by Heather Stanley.*

summer of 1926, together with unusually early snow melts from Canada at the same time, on top of heavy rains falling on central Arkansas, drove the Arkansas River to flood stage in 1927 and eventually burst the dirt levees that held back both the Mississippi and Arkansas Rivers.

When the waters finally receded in August 1927, the death toll was thought to be as many as 127 Arkansans. The state suffered major setbacks and losses in agriculture and industry, and thousands of citizens were homeless.

Floodwaters have played a major role in the shaping of Arkansas's physical and psychological topography. Hopefully, modern understanding and technology will prevent these tragedies from taking such an extreme toll ever again. Amen.

5

Forgotten History in Black and White

Arkansas is located in the southern region of the United States of America. It shares a border with a total of six states, and its eastern border is defined by the Mississippi River. It has a remarkable diversity of geography, from mountains in the Ozark area to the eastern lowlands along the Mississippi River. The most populous city of Little Rock is also its capital and is located near the exact center of the state.

The state topography runs a full range, from mountains and valleys to thick, natural forests and fertile plains. Its lowlands are better known as the Delta and Grand Prairie regions. The Arkansas Delta is a flat landscape of rich alluvial soils that have been formed by the repeated flooding of the Mississippi.

The Delta is intersected by a unique geographical form called Crowley's Ridge. The ridge rises from 250 to 500 feet above the alluvial plain and runs along many of the major towns in eastern Arkansas. With so much fertile land, Arkansas is an agricultural powerhouse!

The northwest section of the state is known as the Ozark Plateau. Its highest point is Mount Magazine in the Ozark Mountains, rising to 2,753 feet above sea level. Arkansas has the only operating diamond mine in the United States. It is one among several states made out of the territory purchased from Napoleon in the Louisiana Purchase. The territory of Arkansas was organized on July 4, 1819. The state of Arkansas was admitted to the Union as the twenty-fifth state.

Arkansas struggles with race issues dating back to the Civil War. A common sight in the parking lots of Walmart stores is a large number of stickers, slogans and artwork still actively depicting the Confederate flag and voicing support for the "old ways" and a lesser number of stickers, slogans and artwork representing the opposite viewpoint. A growing number of these show a line drawn through the Confederate flag artwork with the words "You Lost: Get Over It" emblazoned on top.

This cultural split is still a hot button among old folks gathered to pontificate the meaning of life in barbershops and gas stations and young folks ruminating out loud in coffee shops and bookstores. Arkansas has not excelled in progressive issues like race or gender equality. Arkansas's modern history has been marked by controversy and conflict as social progressivism has crashed headfirst into cultural and religious traditionalism. And some residents are determined never to change.

Arkansas was the thirteenth slave state. The state's cotton culture of the Delta region relied heavily on slave labor, and on the eve of the Civil War in 1860, the number of African American slaves was estimated to be 111,115. That was 25 percent of the state's population. Needless to say, Arkansas seceded from the Union on May 6, 1861.

Under the Military Reconstruction Act, Congress readmitted Arkansas in June 1868. The legislature established universal male suffrage, a public education and other general items designed to improve the state and aid the population. Years later, in 1874, as conservative Democrats began to regain political power, the legislature passed a new constitution.

The Ku Klux Klan made its formal debut in Arkansas exactly one month to the day after liberated slaves were given the right to vote. This organization, while denounced by most, is still a point of pride for a surprising number of folks.

The coming of the railroads not only improved the ability of farmers to get crops to market but also brought new development into new parts of the state, including the Ozarks. At the end of the nineteenth century, Eureka Springs in Carroll County grew to ten thousand people as a tourist destination and the fourth-largest city in the state. Its newly constructed elegant resort hotels and spas were planned around the springs. The water of those springs became famous all over the world as having healing properties.

In the post–Civil War era, Arkansas grew in economics and industry, in politics and social order. Slowly, things began to change and evolve, but despite its growth, to this very day, major highways bypass Arkansas, no major airline uses it as a hub and even its biggest city is called "Little" in its name! The slow growth coupled with a resistance to external and internal forces for change left the state in a bad way as the modern era took shape around it.

In 1954, the legal case of *Brown v. Board of Education* gave rise to the now legendary "Little Rock Nine." The nine were a group of African American students who wanted to enroll in Little Rock's Central High School in order to integrate the student body. The events surrounding the students became a national crisis that put the spotlight of the burgeoning civil rights movement on Arkansas.

In May 1955, the Little Rock School Board adopted the Blossom Plan. The plan set stages for Central High School to be integrated by the end of 1957. The plan then called for integration to carry over to all the lower grade levels within six years. This plan had a clause that allowed students to transfer to another school if they became the minority race. Hence, it was believed everything would remain status quo, despite the plan's stated goals.

The NAACP filed a lawsuit over this apparent contradiction. The federal courts upheld the Blossom Plan as legal and acceptable. So in 1957, nine black students made their way to the school to enroll. Hearing of this plan, Governor Orval Faubus called in the Arkansas

National Guard and gave it the task of keeping the nine out of the school.

When the students arrived on school grounds on September 4, they were met by jeering crowds of segregationists and the National Guard troops who dutifully turned them back from the school's entrances. Taunted and spat upon, the student went home and waited another two weeks.

The federal government ordered Faubus to stop obstructing their enrollment; the nine returned on September 23 and entered the building as increasingly unruly crowds outside chanted, "Two, four, six, eight, we ain't gonna integrate." Before enrollment could be completed, however, the Little Rock police removed them from the premises, saying they feared they would be unable to control the protesting crowds.

President Dwight Eisenhower called the actions in Arkansas "disgraceful" and continued to try to force Faubus to cooperate. Faubus skillfully managed to elude three phone calls from the president.

Finally, the president called in 1,200 members of the army and took the additional step of putting the Arkansas National Guard under federal orders. On September 25, the troops escorted the nine students into the building and on to their classes.

Eventually, the troops had to be withdrawn from the school, but the harassment of the students continued. The Little Rock Nine paved the way for integration to move forward in Arkansas. But the resistance to change was so strong that, despite the victory of the Little Rock Nine, voters decided to close all four high schools in the city for the rest of the year in an effort to stop any further desegregation.

Arkansas voted Democratic in twenty-three consecutive presidential elections from the time of Reconstruction until 1964. During the years of civil rights unrest, political alignments changed to resist progressive legislation. Arkansas voted for George Wallace, a third party candidate, in 1968. Arkansas has since gone Republican seven out of ten times, with the exceptions of Bill Clinton and Jimmy Carter. In 2008, Arkansas went for John McCain over Barack Obama. Obama handily won the election and became America's first African American president.

6

It Came from the Natural State

Arkansas has had its fair share of mysterious creatures that have crawled from the bogs, forests and rice fields. Here are some of the most famous. At least one is certifiably real.

Big Arky

Big Arky is the name given to an alligator captured in Arkansas. This spectacular specimen measured just over thirteen feet long, weighed over five hundred pounds and became a famous attraction for the state. He was, at the time of his capture, believed to be the largest such gator in the western hemisphere. That was the summer of 1952.

Arky was captured in a flooded pasture near Yellow Creek, west of the town of Hope, Arkansas. His captor was a man named Ed Jackson. Mr. Jackson discovered Arky just prior to potentially losing a leg to him. Shocked and unsure what to do with a thirteen-foot alligator in his pasture, Mr. Jackson called on his neighboring friends to lend a hand with this amphibious anomaly.

The team of rural wranglers finally settled on a plan of wrapping Big Arky in a cable attached to a tractor. The tractor was then able to drag the creature out of the pasture. The question now confronting our unintentional wildlife experts was quite simply: where do you take a thirteen-foot cable-wrapped, tractor-dragged alligator?

The answer, of course, was the city of Hope, Arkansas's public children's pool. The newspaper report states that it took seven strong men a total of forty-five minutes to transfer Big Arky to the Little Rock Zoo. This change of venue was no doubt a big relief to the children in the city of Hope.

Marlin Perkins of TV's *Mutual of Omaha's Wild Kingdom* was on hand to assist in every non-life-threatening way he could. This usually involved sending his long-suffering assistant, Jim, into harm's way. The result of all this attention was that Big Arky became famous. He had major celebrity buzz and drew over three thousand people to the zoo his first day on display. Arky was an attraction for the zoo for the next eighteen years.

So beloved was Arky that he made the news when he contracted a vitamin D deficiency and was cured by sun lamps and cod liver oil. When Arky was very old and

The final remains of Big Arky. He now resides in the Arkansas State University Museum in Jonesboro. *Photo by Heather Stanley.*

refused to eat well, he was force fed by the zoo staff. He finally died of humiliation in 1970.

Prior to his death in 1970, Little Rock Zoo patrons started up a memorial fund to preserve his memory. Well, actually, they wanted to preserve more than his memory. He was stuffed, mounted and displayed in the reptile house. Arky was passed around from place to place over the years. He currently resides in the main hall of the Arkansas State University museum. The good news is that this keeps him from ever again suffering the indignity of being dragged behind an Arkansas tractor.

THE FOUKE MONSTER: SMILE WHEN YOU SAY THAT

In May 1971, twenty-five-year-old Bobby Ford told the Fouke constable's office that he heard screams on his property. When he went to see what was wrong, he was attacked by a seven-foot-tall ape-man with glowing red eyes! This was the beginning of the reign of fame for the town of Fouke.

Oh, and before we go any further, allow me to clarify that the proper pronunciation is "fow-k" (sorry). It is a small, strange town of eight hundred people located just outside Texarkana.

Within weeks of Mr. Ford's fantastic monster report, there were stories that the same beast had been seen back in 1963, and three brand-new sightings were called in saying the creature was seen crossing Highway 71. Sadly, the lingering question of "Why did the Fouke monster cross the road?" remains unanswered.

That summer, as Fouke Fever and Monster Mania swelled amongst the area's population, an archaeologist named Frank Schambach from Southern State College came to examine some huge three-toed footprints. The results of his investigation underscored the uncanny similarities in the spellings of both Fouke and Fake.

In the end, no monster was ever found, a handful of locals were fined for fraudulent calls to the police and that should have been the end of the "Fouke Monster," but this is Bizarrkansas. Soon, a real monster was released on the simple townspeople: Arkansas filmmaker Charles B. Pierce.

The year 1972 brought with it the filming of *The Legend of Boggy Creek*. Mr. Pierce, a Texarkana resident and the project's producer, suggested that his movie would garner some Oscar nominations. He cast local residents and shot his low-budget monster movie in the authentic locations in order to re-create the not-so-terrifying events as they actually might have happened.

The movie is now a cult classic regarded as a pioneering work in the no-budget "almost documentary" drama genre. Mr. Pierce and his monster movie have earned twice their weight in popcorn on the drive-in circuit and most importantly give the world a reminder of Arkansas wherever discount DVDs are sold. The film did not garner an Oscar nomination.

The White River Monster:
Of Course It Would Be White

The original reports of the White River monster were made in the year of our lord 1937 by Negro farmers on the Bateman Plantation six miles outside the thriving burg of Newport, Arkansas.

Soon after that, Mr. Bateman himself contacted a Dr. Graves from the Arkansas Game and Fish Commission claiming to have seen the creature. He inquired about the possible nature of the unknown beast, its potential origin and how to address the issue from a scientific perspective. He also requested permission to blow it out of the river with dynamite. His request was denied, but the fame of the creature began to grow.

Crowds gathered, and belief in the monster became unshakable even though no one had captured it, photographed it or otherwise proved or disproved its existence outright. White River monster fever took hold of the town, and everyone wanted a way to get involved. Admittedly, there wasn't a lot to do in Newport in 1937. There's not a lot to do there today, for that matter.

Locals constructed a rather hilarious assortment of giant "monster catching" nets. Each of these nets embodied a unique idea about the monster and how to render it helpless. Even more amazing than the net innovations was a gentleman who created a homemade deep-sea diving suit. Or in this case, a not-very-deep-river diving suit made from various household gadgets. In the end, all the effort and risk availed nothing in regard to finding and apprehending the White River monster.

Eventually, interest in the monster and the lack of evidence for it settled down and was more or less forgotten; that is, until 1971, when reports of the White River monster began again. What strange events could possibly explain the monster's return after more than forty years?

Theories vary, but my money says it has something to do with the fact that the aforementioned Fouke monster craze began six months earlier. After all, why should a nowhere place like Fouke have a monster and a metropolitan center like Newport not have one?

In July, several sets of three-toed footprints were found. This news attracted a legion of "experts" from all over the country, and they rushed in to examine these footprints. On July 14, the CBS Evening News rolled into town to report on the discovery. Speculation grew and opinions differed, but in the end the monster remained a mystery. Still, the amateur explorations continued.

Like long-awaited heroes arriving on the scene just in time, Arkansas's leaders jumped in to protect the persecuted beast. In 1973, the state senate appointed a stretch of the White River as an official river monster habitat. The exact language of the bill states that it is "unlawful to kill, molest, trample or harm the White River Monster while in its native refuge."

One has to assume that word of this action spread quickly in monsterdom and that other creatures have eagerly relocated to Arkansas for its open-minded acceptance of the downtrodden and outcast.

Even more amazing, the White River monster became the subject of an episode of Animal Planet's *Lost Tapes* television program in 2008. This is a show exploring rumored crypto-zoological creatures using cheaply rendered re-creations of witness encounters with the phantom beasts. On this program, the White River monster is credited with folklore that dates back to the

Civil War. In fact, it cites old stories that the monster aided the Confederacy. Well, of course it did. It came from Arkansas.

HEBER SPRINGS WATER PANTHER

The water panther, so they say, is a mix between a puma and a Bigfoot. The legends claim the creature can breathe on land and under water. Yes, I said a puma and a Bigfoot.

It is described as man-like with lots of fur. Its most striking feature is the "hellish scream" it emits whilst roaming about the greenery of Greer's Ferry Lake. There are no known photos of the water panther. Oddly, the water panther has not been sighted in recent years. If you find yourself in Heber Springs and want to inquire about the water panther, it will be necessary for you to speak in the native tongue of an Arkansan. Panther is pronounced "pain-ther." Now you won't feel silly when you ask someone about it!

PETER BOTTOM CAVE MONSTER
(WRITE YOUR OWN JOKE HERE...)

Once upon a time, a doctor was wanted for murder. The doctor managed to live and hide in the valley of Peter Bottom for nearly twenty years. Peter Bottom is a lush area outside the town of War Eagle in northwest Arkansas.

Eventually, the good doctor was captured, brought to justice, sentenced for his crimes and...found to be completely insane. Before he died in 1960, he asked that news reporters be brought in to hear his incredible story.

What he told them was not the story of his crimes but the tale of a fearsome man-like creature living in the valley. He warned that no one should wander into that area. Ever!

As you might imagine, the fact that he was insane and died in a mental institution cast doubt on the story, which received only nominal space in the state's newspapers.

And then, in 1966, two adventuresome young men rode into Peter Bottom and encountered a frenzied man fleeing the area by tractor while shouting dire warnings not to go into the valley. But oh, foolish youth, they rode into the valley, tied up their horses and proceeded to explore on foot. They would soon come face-to-face with what drove the good doctor mad and caused the last person they saw to use a tractor's highest-speed gear while leaving the fields.

At first, they saw what they believed to be the corpse of a horse or cow. It looked like a large lump of white lying in the field. They approached the mass when, much to their dismay, it rose up and turned to face them. Most lumps of hay do not possess this capacity.

The next thing they knew, they were eye-to-eye with a large man-like creature covered in white fur. The hulking

A natural spring cavern. Arkansas was at one time known as the "Hot Water State." Its most famous water-based city is Hot Springs. *Photo by Heather Stanley.*

man-beast then began to move in the direction of our two adventurers. The strangest aspect of this encounter seems to be that while walking toward our heroes, the hell-spawned critter reportedly gave off a strange mechanical beeping sound.

Luckily, our heroes managed to run away, escaping the clutches of the monster, and lived to tell the tale in barbershops, diners and newspaper offices around town.

The monster was never seen again, but there have been reports of dead bodies and mutilated cattle found in the cave. To this day, there are many who believe that in the darkest depths of the Peter Bottom Cave lives the Ozark yeti.

UFOs

Arkansas has had its fair share of encounters with things from other worlds. One of the most famous extraterrestrial events in recent history dates to January 2007. It was then that a retired United States Air Force colonel named Brian Fields photographed two UFOs hovering above his house in Van Buren.

Mr. Fields told his story and shared his pictures with the press. He described lights that "were not of this world" and felt it was his duty to come forward with his best evidence.

He testified that the lights on the spacecrafts appeared and disappeared a number of times and that at one point, as many as four or five lights shone out in a triangular configuration, while sometimes they were stacked vertically.

Fields flew F-16 fighter jets for the military for nearly thirty-two years. He contends that the lights were not possibly from any kind of earthly manufactured aircraft. He identified them as "some kind of energy or something." It's the "or something" part that still fascinates some UFO enthusiasts.

One of the most photographed natural attractions in the state is Pivot Rock in Carroll County. It's right out of a Road Runner cartoon. *Photo by Heather Stanley.*

Arkansas's leading group of UFO enthusiasts meets in Fayetteville and is part of an information-sharing group known as Mutual UFO Network, or MUFON for short. There are a growing number of people watching the skies in the Natural State.

While Mr. Fields's encounter is a contemporary one, Arkansas has a long history of UFO sightings, and the very eccentric town of Eureka Springs hosts an annual springtime UFO conference.

Interestingly enough, I once had the personal experience of giving a business presentation in Eureka Springs. During the course of the presentation, I was informed that a contingency of people in the town believes that aliens not only landed generations ago but also are the reason the spring water has mysterious healing properties. And furthermore, they contend that some of these aliens still live beneath the city in the spring caverns.

7

Forgotten Tales of Bizarrkansans

Arkansas is often more than one thing at a time. Just like with real people, it isn't as simple as wearing a particular label or hitching to a familiar stereotype. So we now offer you the story of some larger-than-life personalities. They are embedded on both sides of modern culture and the moral standards of their time. How wrong or right they are—or were—depends on the perspective of the individual historian.

These characters lived during times of change for both Arkansas and the nation. None was native Arkansan, but they found the state to be a welcome place for their unorthodox enterprises and personal beliefs. Please keep your hands inside the ride at all times and your tray table in its full upright and locked position. Here we go...

Albert Pike, Grand Supreme Enigma

Albert Pike was a Renaissance man. He was a special kind of Renaissance man, the kind that would flourish, bloom and reach for glory during the Civil War era of Arkansas. He was a warrior, politician, judge, writer, poet and, depending on whom you believe, one of the founders of the Ku Klux Klan. Pike was a thinker and a stinker, and herein for your enjoyment is a brief overview of the man and his claims to fame.

His colorful history is the stuff of legends among the world's active conspiracy buffs. A quick search of the Internet will present you with mountains of information that grant Mr. Pike everything ranging from saint and prophet status to that of Lucifer's incarnate right arm on earth. There is no chance that this account of Mr. Pike won't anger someone. To those defenders of the "Pikester," I respectfully say that you must admit the guy was a piece of work.

I like to picture him sitting on a burned-out tree stump at the end of the Civil War. He is angry and distracted as he nervously contemplates the meaning of the South's total defeat. Deep down inside, he bristles at the thought of the eventual premiere of *Gone With the Wind* and the popularity of R&B music. That is my eternal vision of Albert Pike. The facts were these:

Albert Pike was born in Boston, Massachusetts, on December 29, 1809. He was one of six children attributed to Mr. Benjamin Pike and Sarah Andrews.

He attended public schools in Byfield, Newburyport and Framingham, Massachusetts. Young Albert received an exceptional education that grounded him in classical and contemporary literature, Hebrew, Latin and Greek. He passed the examination required for entry into Harvard at the age of sixteen. Albert had smarts! He became a practicing lawyer, and as such, he played a significant role in the early courts and politics of Arkansas prior to the Civil War.

Pike was very active politically in the Whig Party before giving his allegiance to the Know-Nothing Party. He eagerly joined the Southern half of the Civil War argument as a brigadier general on November 22, 1861. Pike demonstrated a great appetite for war and the cause of Dixie.

His superiors took notice of this devoted, capable son of the South and quickly gave him a difficult task. Pike was given charge of the Indian Territory and was asked to recruit, train and make ready for war three Confederate divisions of Indian cavalry. Albert Pike rose to the challenge and gathered and trained his men. In his notes, he proudly states that most of these Indians belonged to the "civilized tribes." The true dedication of these "civilized tribes" to the Confederacy was questionable at best.

Regardless, Pike's soldiers won the day at the Battle of Pea Ridge in March. As Southern pride was rising and the celebration beginning, an unexpected counterattack sent the unit into complete and utter chaos and disorder.

This is a restored Civil War cannon from the Battle of Pea Ridge. It now proudly sits in front of the Pea Ridge Battlefield Museum. *Photo by Kirby Suggins.*

A short time after the Pea Ridge incident, Pike was confronted with the accusation that his troops had gone wild, abandoned the Confederacy and gone on their own independent warpath during the heat of the counterattack. Reports came back to haunt Pike that his men actually scalped other soldiers in the field. "Civilized tribes," he said!

Now, given the nature of his troops, it might be understandable that such an unexpected incident might happen. Albert did not relinquish his stance on the moral high ground over the actions of these men. After all, the behavior of each of these Indian men was beyond his personal control. However, he was also charged with absconding and mismanaging money and many other resources. Upon hearing this charge, and believing that his arrest was imminent, Pike quickly jumped off the moral high ground and beat a path of escape into the familiar hills of Arkansas.

In what can only be called a bold move, he mailed in his resignation from the army on July 12. By early November, Albert Pike's hiding places had been found, and he was arrested on charges of treason and insubordination. Pike was taken from his beloved Arkansas and imprisoned in Warren, Texas.

One of the things that imparts to Pike, and other historical figures like him, such iconic stature is that on one or more occasions, the universe seemed to line up behind him. What happened next can only be considered one of those occasions.

When Pike went to trial, the wartime mail he sent many months before continued its very slow journey to its destination. In what can only be considered a bizarre twist, his July resignation was received and accepted by the War Office on November 11, and Pike was notified that he could return to Arkansas.

Pike went on to become instrumental in the development of the Order of the Free Masons within the state. He is also alleged to have helped start the Ku Klux Klan, along with Nelson Bedford Forrest. This, however, is gray area, or perhaps we should call it "blue and the gray" area.

The *Washington Post* plainly identified Albert Pike as the chief judicial officer of the Klan in 1905. The Klan itself lists Pike as chief judicial officer in its vintage promotional literature. The Klan publication entitled *Knights and Women of the Ku Klux Klan—1925* features a photograph of Pike standing shoulder-to-shoulder with Nathan Bedford Forrest.

The fact that Pike's own son offered the use of his father's portrait for inclusion in a written history of the Klan is reason enough to believe in his Klan connections.

There is another source that might tie him to that organization: his own unapologetically racist writings. For instance, this little gem in a Pike editorial that appeared in the *Tennessee Daily Appeal* on April 16, 1868:

> *With Negroes for witnesses and jurors, the administration of justice becomes a blasphemous mockery. A Loyal League of Negroes can cause any white man to be arrested, and can prove any charges it chooses to have made against him...The disenfranchised people of the South...can find no protection for property, liberty or life, except in secret association...We would unite every white man in the South into one great Order of Southern Brotherhood, with an organization complete, active, vigorous, in which a few should execute the concentrated will of all, and whose very existence should be concealed from all but its members.*

Today, advocates of the Klan embrace Mr. Pike as a leader, while the Masonic Lodge denies and omits record of his involvement in that famous organization. This is likely because, later in life, Pike became a national leader and figurehead for the lodge.

Pike wrote poetry his entire life. Most of his poems mix his narrow worldview with religious overtones. Here is a sample from his poem "Dixie":

> *How the South's great heart rejoices*
> *At your cannon's ringing voices!*
> *For faith betrayed and pledges broken,*
> *Wrongs inflicted, insults spoken*
> *Strong as lions, swift as eagles,*
> *Back to their kennels hunt these beagles!*
> *Cut the unequal bonds asunder!*
> *Let them hence each other plunder!*
> *Swear upon your Country's altar*
> *Never to submit or falter,*
> *Till the spoilers are defeated,*
> *Till the Lord's work is completed.*
> *Halt not till our Federation*
> *Secures among earth's Powers its station!*
> *Then at peace, and crowned with glory,*
> *Hear your children tell the story!*

OK, so that's not exactly the story the children will actually tell, but hey, you have to admit he was sincere about his causes. Despite the Klan controversy, Pike did leave his mark on history and has been memorialized in some unusual and unexpected ways.

The Masonic Lodge erected a statute of him in 1901 in Washington, D.C. This gives him the honor of being the only Confederate general to have a standing monument in the nation's capital. No doubt, his connection to fraternal groups embedded in Washington brought this remarkable honor to bear.

The first highway between Hot Springs, Arkansas, and Colorado Springs, Colorado, is named the Albert Pike Highway. We wonder how he would feel about so many diverse races and colors of people, not to mention non-Masons, kicking across his asphalt on a daily basis.

The Albert Pike Memorial Temple in Little Rock is a Masonic showplace, while his Little Rock home now ironically serves as the Arts Center Community Gallery, a multipurpose gallery in which local and regional art is shown. That last one makes us happy inside. Now where's my deluxe edition of *Gone With the Wind*?

CARRY A. NATION: SELF-APPOINTED "JOAN OF OZARK"

The story of Carry Nation reads like the script of a made-for-TV movie that could only air on a network that positioned itself somewhere between Fox News, Lifetime and Trinity Broadcasting.

Carrie Moore was born on November 25, 1846, in Garrard County, Kentucky, to George and Mary Moore. George Moore owned and operated a southern plantation fully equipped with slaves. Mary Moore suffered a form of mental illness that eventually caused her to believe she was a lady-in-waiting to the queen of England and, still later, that she actually was the queen. Mother ultimately came to divide her time between being the queen and acting like a weather vane. She was the mother to six children, including Carrie.

OK, So Carrie was off to a bit of a weird start. Perhaps fate would be kind and surround her with stable people and circumstances that would afford her a quiet and peaceful life experience. Perhaps her adulthood would yield the well-rooted sanity and love that was missing from her childhood. Perhaps Carrie would rise up to care for others who might have been confused and damaged by emotional illness in their backgrounds too.

I'm assuming you have read enough of the stories in this book already to know that none of those things is going to happen. Oh no. Carrie would instead follow a path that would cause her to become an international celebrity. She

Previous page: Carry named her hatchets Faith, Hope and Charity. She claimed that using a hatchet to smash up saloons instead of a rock was the only good idea she got from her marriage to David Nation. *Original artwork by Jonathan Stanley.*

would be hailed as a champion of morals and religious fervor, hated as a criminal, mocked as a crazy person and made the subject of countless newspaper editorials, books and silent movies. She would be a star on the vaudeville circuit and a prolific author and publisher. She would be debated, disputed and eventually the model for a commercial vinegar bottle long before the familiar shape of Mrs. Butterworth. To this day, Carrie Nation finds her name dropped for laughs in TV sitcoms, mentioned for bonus points amongst savvy history buffs and on loan to a female rock band.

So just what chain of events and cultural shifts made the little girl with the disturbed mother into one of history's greatest enigmatic personalities? Two personified entities: Johnny Reb and Johnny Barleycorn.

As the Civil War broke out, Carrie's father relocated the family (including Queen Mary) to Texas. Along the way, they came to stop near the Pea Ridge battlefield in Benton County, Arkansas. Carrie became very ill during the stop. (It is endlessly fascinating to me that Pea Ridge was the location of the military "glory moment" of our previous subject, Albert Pike. Soak that in for a moment. Albert Pike was leading battle with his civilized Indian troops while Carrie and her family took rest in the same location. These two titans of bizarre history trod the same Arkansas ground for a brief time.)

After her recovery, Carrie Moore married a physician named Charles Gloyd in 1867. Her parents disapproved of the marriage, knowing that Dr. Gloyd was an alcoholic. Apparently, they kept this vital bit of insight to themselves, leaving Carrie to discover it on her own.

The marriage was most unhappy. The couple's time together was marked by alternating tides of great affection and furious conflict. An only child, a girl named Charlien, was born to the Gloyds. The girl would shortly manifest signs of mental disability. Rather than recall her own immediate family's mental health issues, Carrie made an earth-shaking shift in her rationale for the girl's problems. Carrie blamed the child's troubles on her husband's drinking.

And drink he did! Mr. Gloyd was a textbook alcoholic. He began, like thousands of other men from that era, while in the army during the Civil War. Drinking was a distraction and an accepted pastime for soldiers. Truth be told, the Civil War set the stage for the battle of the bottle with which America would wrestle until the end of Prohibition.

Charles left the army and began a promising career as a doctor. He was well regarded in his town and kept his drinking in the background. With his war buddies dispersed, he found new drinking partners at the Masonic Lodge. Carrie would come to insist that the lodge was an evil organization that led men to destruction and into darkness rather than toward God's light.

Dr. Gloyd began a serious descent into his drinking problem after marrying Carrie. He realized he was a lost soul and incapable of dealing with his addiction. Remember, at this time in history, there was no AA meeting to attend, no support group to find and no rehab program to sign up for. Alcoholism was America's postwar epidemic. Carrie's husband beame so useless and pathetic that she eventually packed up her daughter and left him. Gloyd died within weeks of her departure.

Carrie Gloyd was now a single mother working odd jobs and struggling mightily to get by. She was also now armed with the singular notion of what would become her legendary crusade: that drink was the great enemy of all things good and godly and that it must be eliminated. No discussion, no compromise. Alcohol was her Goliath, and she was God's faithful David, determined to slay the noisy giant!

Carrie married a man named David Nation. David was a newspaper editor and a part-time preacher. He was Carrie's senior by a whopping twenty-nine years. Carrie, having bounced out of an unsatisfying first marriage, desired romance and expressions of love, which the aging Mr. Nation never seemed to adequately provide.

This relationship began to sour over the couple's constant and fierce arguments about religion and theology. Despite David Nation being an ordained minister, Carrie made it clear that she didn't think he was much of a preacher.

During his sermons, she prompted him from the front rows on how to present the message and how to make it more forceful and expressive. Carrie taught Mr.

Nation visual cues based on gestures she would make in the front-row pew. In much the same style as child evangelist Marjoe Gortner would report on his mother, Carrie would coach, cue and prompt the elder statesman for God through his presentations. At times, she would interrupt him and say, "That's enough David. Just stop." Carrie found little satisfaction in married life with Nation and even less in her attempts to transform him into the "spokesman for God" she could see and hear in her own head.

In 1877, David Nation was asked to resign as preacher of his church because of the trouble his wife was making for the entire congregation. Uprooted, the Nation family arrived back in Texas against Carrie's wishes. Carrie would bounce from place to place and wind up back in Kansas.

In lieu of the amorous attention she seemed to have hoped for from her new husband, and feeling uncertain about his calling as a preacher, Carrie began to develop her own spirituality. This development came in the form of visions and callings that seemed to single her out for a mission from God. It was during this time that Carrie felt her call from God to save America from the evils of alcohol. She even changed the spelling of her name from Carrie to Carry and added her middle initial of A. to become the larger-than-life "blood-bought, devil-fought, Bible-bangin' super hero Carry A. Nation." In fact, she copyrighted the term "Carry A. Nation" in Kansas.

She came to believe her calling was literally to Carry A. Nation away from the evils of alcohol. Yes, she believed herself to be "Joan of Ozark."

Now, the way Carry expressed her personal convictions about alcohol was to walk into the nearest establishment serving liquor and pull from her Sunday go-to-meeting purse one or more of the hatchets she named Faith, Hope and Charity and open a can of whoop-axe on everyone and everything in the place.

She smashed the bottles; busted up the mirrors on the wall; chopped chunks out of the bars, tables and walls; broke glasses; and more or less went berserk on the property. And while she performed these acts of personal property destruction, she sang hymns and quoted Bible verses. She would often enter the bar and address the owner, saying, "Good morning destroyer of men's souls!"

Carry took her crusade of smashing on the road and become quite famous as a popular "love her or hate her" character of the day. She was going rogue and making headlines while doing it. Now, this being the Victorian era and her being (a type of) lady, she was largely unhindered in her actions.

Before her years of sensational smashing were over, she would be arrested more than thirty times. Carry used her arrests to stir her followers to moral outrage. Carry's attention-getting tactics were innovative and clever. She was plowing some now familiar ground that protesting iconic cultural figures would utilize to the present day. She also innovated the making of merchandise to fund a divisive cause. She usually raised bail money by selling souvenir hatchets to her fans at live appearances and through the mail. Perhaps without Carry and her little hatchets, there would be no prayer hankies or tiny vials of blessing water sent through the mail by countless evangelists today.

And speaking of sending things through the mail, Carry developed a newsletter called the *Smashers Mail*. It was a small publication sent to supporters for a small donation that was packed with Carry's opinions on all things moral and theological.

Carry seemed to develop more and more unusual ideas about things as her life progressed. Sometimes this would show through the articles found inside the *Smashers Mail*. At one point, she wrote an article called "Mother Nation Speaks to Boys." This article addressed the moral ramifications of what Mother Nation apparently thought all boys were thinking, wanting and doing to themselves and others sexually. She offered unwanted advice to unasked questions. It came across much more like a creepy, unsolicited confession than helpful advice.

So bizarre was this article that the United States Postal Service fined her for sending inappropriate and immoral materials to the public. This, of course, was used by Carry as evidence that the world was against her and didn't want to hear the "hard truths" she preached.

A warm and inviting glow from an altar. *Photo by Heather Stanley.*

There is a vintage photo of Carry that was taken around this time. It was a staged photo intended to promote her appearances in theaters. No one is certain how this particular photo came to be arranged or what prompted it. It remains a very strange visual metaphor for the life and views of Carry Nation.

In this photo, Carry is wearing her usual stern black dress. The unusual part of this picture is what she is doing. Carry is withholding an ice cream cone from the eager mouth of a young man, apparently a theater usher. Her expression is one of intense interest toward the boy, and her free hand is clutching and crushing a rolled-up bit of paper. The imagery of sexual frustration is overwhelming.

This is all the more interesting because Carry was very careful about being photographed at all. She claims she did not like it and found it vain. In her autobiography, she says she only became comfortable with it if her Bible and her axe appeared in the photo with her to represent her high calling and crusade.

Carry spent her years busting up saloons, making speeches and championing the cause of shutting down the manufacture and distribution of alcohol. She was invited to perform as a headliner in vaudeville. When her tour came to a new town, she would go smash a saloon, get bailed out of jail before sundown and return to the theater, where she paced her way through a staged smashing and then give a speech about temperance for sold-out crowds.

Eventually, as Carry grew more and more outrageous, her supporters began to distance themselves from the fiery lady. Her church denomination, political leaders and even the Woman's Christian Temperance Union would step away from her. She came to be seen more and more as a hatchet-wielding crazy lady whose outlandish behavior was not a help to the cause of temperance.

In 1901, David Nation filed for divorce from his now famous globetrotting wife on the grounds of desertion and cruelty. A judge granted the divorce with no contest.

Nation's disabled daughter, Charlien, was committed to the Texas State Lunatic Asylum in 1905. Carry eventually brought her to her new home in Hot Springs, Arkansas. Charlien never measured up to her mother's theology, and the two argued and debated the meaning of life on a regular basis. The girl usually bested her mother's logic. In the end, Charlien lost this argument when Carry decided to send her away again. She would spend the rest of her life alone in an institution.

At sixty years of age, Carry wrote her version of her life's story: *The Use and Need of the Life of Carry A. Nation.* The book was well received by her supporters, renewed her now sagging fame and gave a glimpse into the way Carry saw herself and her tactics.

In 1909, Carry Nation moved to the eclectic Arkansas town of Eureka Springs. She dubbed her house on Steele Street "Hatchet Hall." The big white sign still proudly resides on the home, which for a time was not only her house but also a religious school she called National College. She provided instruction to the female students who took up residence in the house for the fee of ten dollars a month.

Carry was very much taken with the atmosphere of Eureka Springs and become a huge advocate of the famous water from the springs, which many believed could cure all manner of ailments and sorrows. Carry wanted America to drink the much-fabled Eureka Springs water as an alternative to alcohol.

Arkansas actress Meshayla Payne standing in front of Carry Nation's last house, which she named Hatchet Hall. Directly across from the house, now covered with plywood, is the spring that she blew into the mountain wall to generate her own wellspring. *Photo courtesy of Meshayla Payne.*

So much did Carry love the town and its magical water that she is said to have walked out of Hatchet Hall and lobbed a stick of dynamite into a small cave directly across from her front door. Carry said God told her there was a spring inside that cave just for her.

The resulting explosion shot rocks and debris into the narrow street, followed by a freshly opened spring! Postcards of Carry in front of her spring were sold in town for many years. All of this helped spread the mythology and mystic water from Eureka Springs. The water was eventually sold commercially and resulted in the Ozarka Water Company. Ozarka is still popular bottled water, but the current supply comes from Missouri.

Carry ran her school in Hatchet Hall and struggled to regain the fame and attention she once had. She attempted a comeback of sorts, but it was never to see success. Carry was getting older, and her health was deteriorating. She was given to spells and short bouts of weakness. Carry herself likely did not understand the condition she was suffering with. It was about to catch up with her—a condition with which she had coped all her life in silence. This particular condition would come to explain quite a lot about Carry Nation's beliefs and actions.

Ironically, it was Friday 13, 1911, when Carry took the stage in Basin Park in Eureka Springs to give her very last speech. She began to make her familiar points when her speech pattern became segmented and disjointed. The fire seemed to fade from the face of this warrior. The crowd became more captivated by watching the visual transformation of Carry Nation than by the words she continued to speak.

She finished her speech and polite applause broke out, and as she turned to leave the platform, she collapsed into the arms of a friend. The crowd let out a collective gasp as they watched the mighty figure crumble to the ground. The story would surface that her last words to those attending her in the park were: "I hath done what I could."

Carry A. Nation fell into a coma and was transported to a sanitarium in Kansas. It was Leavenworth, Kansas, to be exact. She had no family to attend to her and very little money, so she ended up in this public facility. This facility served Leavenworth Prison as well. Carry regained consciousness and lingered for months before she died in November of that year.

As it turns out, Carry spent her last days in a wing of this care unit that was full of recovering alcoholics. When Carry finally passed away, the hospital listed "nervous exhaustion" as the cause of death. The State of Kansas rejected this as an unacceptable explanation for the cause of death. The official cause was then changed to "heart failure." Years later, the head administrator of the hospital wrote a book about his experiences there and stated that the real cause of death for Carry Nation were complications from congenital syphilis.

The symptoms of congenital syphilis would have included a slow but continual swelling of the brain tissue inside the skull, a collapse of the skeleton material at the bridge of the nose and brow line while the lower jaw expanded, as well as digestive issues.

In many later photos of Carry, we can clearly see the shrinking of her nose and brow line and the wide jaw. Medical journals suggest that the constant swelling of the brain pressing against the skull could in some cases create hallucinations and visions in the sufferer of this disease. Perhaps this explains Carry's religiously fueled visions?

It is important to point out to those who are understandably sympathetic to the crusade against alcoholism that Carry's behavior went much further than protesting liquor. As the years went by, she spoke and acted out against tobacco products; state, federal and local government; fashion clothes for women; sex; and men as a whole. Her compulsion to be against things in which others find joy and pleasure was the reason leaders who first embraced her antics later distanced themselves from her.

She was buried in her mother's family cemetery in Belton, Missouri. Her grave was unmarked until the Women's Christian Temperance Union put up a gravestone with her name and the statement "Faithful to the Cause, She Hath Done What She Could."

If Carry had lived a few years longer, she could have seen Prohibition become law—a poorly thought-out law doomed to failure as a social experiment. And one that created empires for thugs, bootleggers and mob bosses.

Prohibition still stands as evidence that one simply cannot legislate morality.

Hatchet Hall still stands in Eureka Springs. It was once a museum and tourist attraction, but today the hall is once again a private residence. The spring she blasted into the cave across from her house is now covered with a sheet of plywood. Nearby is a spring named after Carry, although fewer and fewer residents are sure which spring is actually Carry's namesake.

An Arkansas newspaper from July 2012 demonstrating that prohibition is still an issue in many parts of the state. Carry would be proud! *Photo by Edward Underwood.*

Carry came from obscurity, rose to international fame and polarized America over moral issues and religious dogma. But in the end, she is a woman who championed the sanctity of marriage but had two failed relationships, called herself the defender of the home but sent her only child away to an institution, preached self-control but destroyed other people's property at will, preached a narrow religious view as the key to joy and peace but seemed to have none and spoke against government-funded programs yet died alone, penniless, in a state-funded hospital.

Not far from the scene of one of her first hatchet-smashing sessions in Wichita, Kansas, a fountain was built in her honor. A few years later, the fountain was destroyed when an out-of-control beer truck ran into and over it.

The story of Carry A. Nation is one of the most uniquely American and Arkansan in all of history. At the time of

Graphic art created for the indie film project *How to Carry A. Nation*, a project your authors are attempting to make about axe-wielding prohibitionist Carry Nation. *Original artwork by Jonathan Stanley.*

this writing, the authors are seeking to make a movie called *How to Carry A. Nation*. It will be the first movie to tell the forgotten tale of Carry Nation.

GERALD K. SMITH: GIVE ME THAT OLD-TIME DERISION

Here again, we have a life that embodies crusader-like passion and single-minded devotion to a cause mixed with a string of hard-to-believe facts. In Smith's case, his larger-than-life adventures left behind a larger-than-life memorial.

In fact, the Christ of the Ozarks statue next to Mr. Smith's grave is among the one hundred tallest statues in the world. It ranks just behind a baker's dozen of other graven images, including some other Jesuses, Lord Vishnus, Shivas, a handful of Marys and the Dallas Zoo's giraffe. But just how does one aspire to be remembered with a sixty-five-foot-tall cement Jesus?

It began on February 27, 1898, in Pardeeville, Wisconsin. Young Smith grew up in Viroqua, Wisconsin, and was ordained as a minister in the Disciples of Christ denomination in 1916. In his career as a preacher, he made radio broadcasts in support of trade unions while calling to task local utility companies.

Smith had already taken the step of melting doctrine with activism. This form of dominion theology would grow to epic proportions during the "moral majority" era of American politics in the 1980s.

The Christ of the Ozarks stands tall and proud on the highest point in Eureka Springs. *Photo by Heather Stanley.*

Smith befriended Huey Long in 1932, and together they created the Share Our Wealth society. The SOW group advocated fixed minimums and maximums on personal wealth and income for all American citizens. During this era, Smith let go of ministry in order to more fully pursue the goals of the SOW society.

But when Huey Long was assassinated in 1935, Smith believed political power brokers staged the killing. He went on to specifically blame the "Roosevelt gang and the New York Jew machine." Smith became a man who told it like he saw it—even if the way he saw it was a bit screwy.

Here is a case in point: it was so obvious to Smith that evil insiders ran so much of the country that it was going to take an outsider, a singular man of courage and conviction, to straighten out the nation, and he was willing to be that man of destiny.

So, Mr. Smith went to Washington and aimed his rhetorical guns at President Dwight Eisenhower. He attacked Ike for his connections to Jews. Among Smith's unusual socio-religious beliefs was that an international council of Jews planned world dominion through World

War II. He outspokenly argued that the Nazi-led holocaust of the concentration camps was an invention of Jewish-owned media.

Our man then took his Share Our Wealth society in the direction of white supremacy. He formed the America First political party and became a member of the Silver Shirts. This was a political activist group based on Hitler's brown shirts organization. He ran as a Republican candidate for the senate in Michigan but lost the primary. At least we can be comforted by the fact that a pro-Nazi, Jew-hating candidate didn't win a Republican primary in Michigan.

One characteristic of Mr. Smith is that whenever he was confronted with a setback or a failure in his ambitions, he simply aimed higher. This consistent trait tells us a great deal about the thinking process involved. In as much as Mr. Smith was a bundle of contradictions, so too were his motives. From his overtly stated religious cause perspective, Smith was simply a man following a higher calling. From a strictly secular perspective, we see him as a man determined to be in charge of something or anything at almost any cost.

Having failed as a senator from Michigan, he ran for president as leader of his own America First Party in 1944. He received a grand total of 1,781 votes. Not a strong showing by any measure.

But armed with endless ambition and a sense of destiny, Smith redoubled his efforts in 1948. He was determined to rise to the highest-elected office in America by running another campaign with his friend Harry Romer as his running mate. The pair offered America the Christian Nationalist Party ticket. After a nail-biting night of election returns, it was revealed that the Smith-Romer team pulled in a spectacular forty-eight total votes.

Smith sat out the next two election cycles to create an ironclad strategy for becoming the president of the United States. In 1956, he received eight write-in votes. This would mark the end of his efforts to become the leader of the free world. He would, however, still endeavor to win hearts and minds to his narrow views of the world.

Smith had invested decades into attempts to get all Nazi war criminals from the Nuremberg Trials released. This was because he believed the Holocaust never happened. It would seem that Smith couldn't see the connection between his personal beliefs and his utter failure as a politician.

Over all these years, Smith had cranked out newsletters to a growing mailing list. His hate-filled rants on religious, political and racial issues were generating quite a bit of heat. Consequently, he decided to relocate someplace where he could operate a bit more under the radar. He chose Eureka Springs, Arkansas.

In the year 1964, Gerald K. Smith began construction of a mind-boggling religious theme park. While the park never completely materialized as it was originally envisioned, its centerpiece did.

The year 1966 saw the now familiar spectacle of the Christ of the Ozarks become a reality—a reality that looms high above this artists' colony of eccentric citizens from its perch of 1,500 feet on top of Magnetic Mountain. Magnetic Mountain is a place famous for some rather mystical, spiritual properties.

It was believed that this highest pinnacle in the city was possessed of a powerful magnetic vortex. This energy vortex reportedly has the power to shift and alter physical properties in humans, nature and inanimate objects to a higher or excited state of being.

Magnetic Spring, located along the road up to Magnetic Mountain, is still a popular spot for tourists taking pictures. The plaque mounted above the basin of water recounts the stories of how dipping a coin, paper clip or other metal object in the water would cause it to become magnetized and stick to other metal surfaces. Not surprisingly, many came to see this spring and its surrounding grounds as a very mystical place.

All of my personal efforts to magnetize an object in the magnetic spring basin have failed. The reason, we are told, is that over time the spring became diluted or that the water feeding the basin is not the original source. There are many such anomalies in Eureka Springs. In the end, however, it may have more to do with the "Tinker Bell principle." Simply stated, once everyone stops believing in the phenomenon, it dies.

Magnetic Springs was touted to have mystical qualities, including the ability to magnetize metal objects that were dipped into the spring well. *Photo by Edward Underwood.*

Regardless of your opinion of the magical waters and the invisible power field, Mr. Smith planted his giant Jesus smack on the top of that land. It was an ambitious undertaking!

Smith arranged to have the statue sculpted by Emmet Sullivan. Emmet's claim to fame was that he served under the top artists who worked on and put the finishing touches on the faces of Mount Rushmore. Contracting Mr. Sullivan allowed Mr. Smith to capitalize on his statue's perfectly combining religion and patriotism into a single symbol.

The ever-present statue has its share of critics, and many locals call it "our milk carton with arms," "Gumby Jesus" and, our favorite, "Big Cement Jeebus." You can catch a glimpse of the statue in the feature films *Elizabethtown* and *Pass the Ammo*, the latter of which was shot entirely in Eureka Springs. Or, better yet, make a trip to Eureka Springs to see it for yourself. That's the only way you can really believe it.

It is believed that one of Smith's longtime benefactors, Wickliffe Draper, ponied up the money for the Christ of the Ozarks statue. Mr. Draper was a man with a cause as well as money. His causes included opposing civil rights of all kinds, a Hollywood blacklist campaign, a compulsory sterilization movement for America and the Back To Africa Repatriation movement.

Smith continued his various newsletters and remained faithful to his views over the years, his giant Jesus statue and Christian rhetoric sitting uneasily next to his divisive social and political ideals.

While the theme park never came to be, an outdoor passion play based on the one created for Oberammergau, Germany, is presented on a stage set adjacent to the statue. The play is the single biggest tourist attraction for Eureka Springs as a whole. Upon the show's opening, Smith took intensive criticism for blatantly anti-Semitic content in the play. Over the years, some changes were made, and today the *Great Passion Play* is embraced by thousands of tourists and church groups that travel hundreds of miles to attend and reattend the program year after year.

This ornate gazebo welcomes you when you enter the world of the *Great Passion Play*. The grounds host not only the play but also a Bible museum, a dinner theater, gift shops, a chunk of the Berlin wall, the Christ of the Ozarks and the Smiths' graves. *Photo by Kevin Underwood.*

In 1976, Gerald K. Smith died of pneumonia. At the time of this writing, he and his wife are buried together next to the statue in a vault that plays prerecorded hymns.

The family has continued to add and expand to the attraction. Growing ever closer to the original concept of a Christian theme park, there is now a Bible museum, a section of the Berlin Wall, a replica of the Old Testament Tabernacle, a dinosaur exhibit that denounces evolution, a dining hall and, of course, a gift shop.

For those who know the back story of how Mr. Smith was considered a leader of anti-Semitism in America, tying himself to controversial views on civil rights and fringe political and social causes, his past casts an ideological shadow over the big statue and the performance about forgiveness and love. For some, it is simply too bizarre to comprehend.

Smith's story is uniquely American and a cozy little chapter in the annals of our beloved Bizarrkansas.

VICTOR MAYFIELD: THE GOOD DOCTOR OF MENA

By now you've come to realize that Arkansas is a place that is very much dominated by its sense of strong moral compass and religious traditions. Part of that tradition is pride in the ability to tell good from evil, right from wrong and the sincere and pure from the scheming and deceptive.

Countless times I've had a fellow Arkansan explain to me that his spiritual gift includes this kind of discernment. This spiritual gift probably has its roots in the natural suspicion of others—suspicion that a stranger arriving in town would create competition in either business or resources or perhaps simply that the stranger might be more talented, more likeable or tell funnier jokes. Consequently, "You ain't from around here, are ya?" is a traditional first-time greeting in many parts of Arkansas.

Casting the suspicious eye of alleged discernment usually appears to be vindicated most of the time. It's like predicting that something bad will happen with the weather before too long. Chances are it will. Likewise, if you are suspicious of someone's character, when hardship or failure comes to that person eventually, you can claim a victory.

There is one set of circumstances that will always vex the reliability of this spiritual gift: those occasions in which all the spiritually attuned locals happen to love and accept the once mysterious outsider.

With that in mind, we present for you now one of the great forgotten tales of Arkansas. We want you to meet the amazing healer from Mena, Dr. Victor Mayfield.

It was a quiet, sunny day in 1918 when a kindly man with a peaceful demeanor arrived in the tiny burg of Mena, Arkansas, in Polk County. Mena is a city that exists because it is nearly somewhere else.

Arthur Edward Stillwell established the town in 1896 as he was building the Kansas City, Pittsburgh and Gulf Railroad through Arkansas. It was a stopping-off place on the way to Port Arthur, where the railroads would converge at stations.

Mr. Stillwell named the town after the nickname of the wife of his friend and business partner Jan DaGeoijen. Mena began because it was almost Port Arthur. Today, it is most known for being almost all the way to several tourist locations, including Talimena Scenic Drive, a National Scenic Byway and Queen Wihelmina State Park.

The Cossatot River, Quachita National Forest and Lake Ouachita are also places over one million tourists pass through Mena to get to.

The town reached its maximum population at just under six thousand people and is famous for two controversies within the state of Arkansas. First, Mena was home to the Commonwealth College. This organization came to Mena in 1924 and quickly polarized people over its alleged ties to and teachings of Communism and Socialism. The most famous student of Commonwealth College came to be Governor Orval Faubus, a man who led his share of controversy in the state when he refused entry of black students into Little Rock's Central High School in the late 1950s.

Mena's other notable five minutes of fame involved some high rollers named George H.W. Bush, George W. Bush and Bill Clinton. The issue was Mena's suspected use as a major drop spot for cocaine trafficking in the late 1980s and beyond. The charges were that powerful men like presidents were conspiring to cover up the fact that America's main supply of cocaine was being airdropped into Mena, Arkansas.

Saline County prosecutor Dan Harmon was convicted of numerous felony charges and sent to prison in 1997. None of the aforementioned high rollers sustained any lasting damage from the whole affair. Long before that very public brouhaha, our story was quietly unfolding amongst the simple townsfolk.

It was back on that quiet, sunny day in 1918 that this oh-so-pleasant man wandered the streets of the town and met some of the locals. He announced to them that he was a physician and was looking for a good town that needed a doctor. Before the day was over, Dr. Victor Mayfield had rented a second-floor space above the Central Meat Market Shoppe located at 709 Main Street.

Over the next weeks and months, the people of Mena wholeheartedly embraced the good doctor. Mayfield's office was always full of local folks and their kids waiting to see this remarkable man. His business grew rapidly due to word of mouth that he had a gentle, reassuring manner that helped take the worry and fear out of visiting a doctor in 1918.

In this little town where everybody knew everybody else, Dr. Mayfield had become an integral part of daily life. And he was a social hit as well. Victor could be seen smoking his pipe and tossing back whiskey shots in the local saloon. He was the town billiards champion and was known to uncork a real ripper of a dirty joke for a few of the select men still standing late at night in the pool hall.

Victor was a smooth operator personally as well. His suits were clean and pressed, and he was always seen in dress clothes, never frumpy casual wear. His complexion was smooth and his skin clear and bright. His hair was always better groomed than that of other men.

He told fascinating tales of his time among the Indians in the western states. He explained that he learned many medicinal secrets from them. In fact, he attributed his fine skin to an Indian remedy that made shaving unnecessary. He also said he was developing new cures and medical ideas from these experiences.

The ladies of the town become quite enamored of the doctor, and the rumor was that some of the Mena widow women went to the doctor without actually being sick just to get an exam and a bit of touching from the most eligible bachelor in town.

Needless to say, within a couple of years, Victor Mayfield had become a respected pillar of the community with a solid reputation as a good man and a fine, trusted healer. He eventually gained the nickname "cancer doctor," as he brought comfort and relief to those suffering with that most grave of diseases. Somehow he instilled a quiet confidence in his patients. He imparted an unspoken sense that everything would be all right now that Dr. Mayfield was here.

Now, as fate would have it, the good doctor himself became very ill in the latter part of 1926. Victor had just turned seventy-nine years old. The people of the town were concerned for him. Concern gave way to out-and-out worry when the great man locked himself in his room and would see no one for days.

Friends called on another nearby doctor, W.C. Vandiver, to reach out to Mayfield and help cure and restore his strength. When finally Dr. Vandiver burst into Mayfield's room, he found Dr. Mayfield lying on the bed wearing a full suit and tie but weak, trembling and barely clinging to life. Mayfield protested against the help that had arrived but was too weak to resist. In a few moments, Vandiver made a discovery that would send shock waves through the town, the state and, in time, the nation.

A closer examination of Dr. Mayfield and the removal of his suit clothes yielded the unmistakable yet unbelievable fact that Victor was Victoria! Yes, it turns out that the most eligible bachelor in Mena was a woman.

The white-hot shock that shot up the spines of the local people resulted in outrage and anger over the deception. After all, they had trusted this man! They told everyone he was all right, that he was good man. It would be very difficult at this point for anyone to argue that their spiritual discernment had always been troubled over the doctor. They were embarrassed that they had been completely fooled. And by a woman!

There were no softer notes sounded about how Mayfield had been a good doctor and a friend to everyone. All that remained was the bitter taste of being wrong about the gender identity of this previously beloved pillar of the community.

The news made the local papers, and then the Little Rock news picked it up, and it was a sensation. Shortly, the Mayfield scandal story broke nationwide. Now, with so many reporters looking to keep the buzz alive, the search was on for any and all information about who

Victoria Mayfield really was. And that's where this story gets even more bizarre.

The search for answers simply brought more questions. Investigative sources found evidence that Mayfield had been married twice to other women from different states at the same time. Another story surfaced that Mayfield was arrested for fraud years before and that she was believed to have died in a suspicious fire in the jail. Perhaps the most intriguing story that surfaced was that Mayfield had been employed as an undercover spy for the government in Washington, D.C.

Mayfield did recover a measure of health, and as the atmosphere toward her in Mena was so very toxic, she left Arkansas for what she claimed was her home state of Nebraska.

Unfortunately, Mayfield was broke, and in as much as Nebraska had no genuine documentation of his/her citizenship, when she ran out of money, she returned to Mena to be a ward of the state. She asked a photographer from St. Louis for ten dollars in exchange for allowing a picture.

Victor, whose real name was finally discovered to be Mary, died in 1929. She was buried in an unmarked pauper's grave in, according to her last wish, a man's suit of clothes. The ceremony was performed at her request by a woman named Fannie Vise.

Remember the story of Dr. Mayfield as ironclad proof that in a small town like Mena, everybody knows everyone else...or at least they think they do! In the end, the good doctor put a new spin on the meaning of being a real ladies' man.

8

Outdated Arkan-laws

- Schoolteachers who bob their hair will not get raises.
- The Arkansas River can rise no higher than the Main Street Bridge in Little Rock.
- Alligators cannot be kept in bathtubs (tell that to Big Arky!).
- A man can legally beat his wife, but no more than once during a month.
- Honking a car horn at a sandwich shop after 9:00 p.m. is illegal.
- It is unlawful to walk your cow down Main Street in Little Rock after 1:00 p.m. on Sunday.
- Dogs may not bark after 6:00 p.m.

9

SOME ARKANSAS HEROES

With all these forgotten tales of the strange, quirky, offbeat and outright weird people, places and things, let us not forget that Arkansas has likewise produced some brilliant champions and leaders as well. The same open spaces and wild-card freedom mentality that fueled the oddball also gave room for the rise of genius. Enjoy.

ALMEDA JAMES RIDDLE: OZARK HUMAN JUKEBOX

Almeda James's long and unlikely life began on November 21, 1898, in Cleburne County. At the tender young age of eighteen, she married a man with the colorful name of H. Price Riddle. The year was 1918. The couple began a family near the town of Heber Springs. An unexpected touch of tragedy was about to change Almeda's life forever.

In 1926 a tornado destroyed the town and took the lives of her husband and one of her four children.

Almeda pressed on as a single mother, working and scraping by as best she could. The years were not kind to the fatherless family. Though her world was always falling apart, Almeda kept two things intact: her faith and, literally, a song in her heart.

Almeda became a tribute to the best of what humanity can be. She struggled but never stumbled. She ached but never complained. She was outmatched by the world at every turn, but she never gave up and never let that song in her heart end. And after years of this brave and patient existence, a miracle was about to happen.

It's almost as if that brilliant spark of human determination and hope acted like a radio signal. Her faith and that song became an unseen searchlight that drew the most unlikely of outcomes directly to her. The front porch of her mother's house was about to transform into launch pad that would take this long-suffering lady higher than she could have ever imagined.

In 1952, the first of the so-called ballad hunters—academics who championed traditional folk music as a means of understanding grass-roots American history—found Almeda on that front porch in Greer's Ferry.

Professor John Quincy Wolf of Southwestern College in Memphis found Almeda still living and working as sole provider for her aging mother and her grown children. He also found more than he ever imagined or hoped for!

Inquiring about the songs she sang around the house and during her work, he was able to discern that many of the songs that played endlessly in Almeda's heart and mind dated back to seventeenth-century England, Ireland and Scotland. Almeda Riddle had her extended family's immigrant history locked away in her memory in the form of songs—songs she must have heard as a baby and all through her young adulthood. And she hadn't forgotten a word.

As it turns out, her family had imparted to her an unassuming form of wealth—a wealth of culture and history in the form of these songs tucked away in her mind. Her years of hardship kept her drawing on those songs for the hope, values and encouragement. Almeda was a walking, talking treasure chest.

Professor Wolf and his team began making countless recordings of Almeda singing each and every one of the old songs she remembered. There seemed to be no end to the number of songs she could perfectly recall. This is how she earned the nickname the "human jukebox." In fact, it is estimated that her memories of ballads, church songs, children's songs and such make up the largest single repertoire ever documented from a single source.

Thirty years later, the National Endowment for the Arts would pay tribute to Riddle as the "great lady of Ozark balladry." As it turns out, Almeda could not only recall any and all of these songs, but she could also perform them perfectly at will.

By 1959, rock-and-roll was taking over American culture, but somewhere off in a dusty corner of Arkansas, Almeda was responding to the request to make an album of her favorite songs. At the age of sixty-two, she was suddenly in demand. She began touring, recording and bringing her old songs to people everywhere.

In the early '60s, Riddle was considered a prominent figure in the American folk music revival and was sharing the spotlight with young whippersnappers like Bob Dylan, Pete Seeger and Joan Baez. Riddle became a top-earning concert attraction at folk festivals from coast to coast.

Riddle recorded over two hundred songs, and fifty were transcribed into her book, *Almeda Riddle's Book of Ballads*. The book not only documented the songs but also came to challenge the idea that the old hill people were uneducated and unskilled in music. It also created the awareness that folk songs were a method of transferring moral lessons, information and oral history.

Her titles kept changing as promoters made bigger and bigger business from the swelling interest in folk music. She was billed as "Granny Riddle," "Folk Artist of the Arkansas Ozarks" or, simply, "The Balladeer." Riddle was happy to dole out her songs to one and all as long as she could. The great lady of Ozark folk songs closed out her career in 1984 at the Ozark Folk Center in Mountain View, Arkansas. She performed "From Jerusalem to Jericho" along with Mike Seeger.

In December of that year, Almeda moved into a nursing home in Heber Springs and died two years later. Within two years of her passing, another collection of her songs and recordings was released, her songbook updated and a thirty-minute public television special produced about her life story. God bless ya, Almeda, and thanks for the music!

HATTIE OPHELIA WYATT CARAWAY:
YESTERDAY'S WOMAN OF TOMORROW

Hattie Caraway was the first woman elected to the U.S. Senate, the first woman to preside over the Senate, the first woman to chair a Senate committee and the first woman to preside over a Senate hearing.

She served from 1932 to 1945 and was a strong supporter of President Franklin D. Roosevelt's economic recovery legislation during the Great Depression.

Hattie was born on February 1, 1878, in Bakersville, Tennessee. The family relocated to Hustburg, where she eventually enrolled in Ebenezer College. Still later, she transferred to Dickson Normal College in Dickson and received a BA in 1896. She married Thaddeus Horatius Caraway on February 5, 1902, and the couple set up a home in the city of Jonesboro, Arkansas.

Mr. Caraway was elected to the U.S. House of Representatives for the Democrats in 1912. He served the State of Arkansas in the House until March 2, 1921. He then won a Senate seat in 1920 and served from March 4, 1921, up to his untimely and unexpected death in 1931.

And then the truly unexpected happened: Arkansas governor Harvey Parnell asked Hattie to fill her husband's Senate seat on November 13, 1931. She was sworn in on December 8, 1931, confirmed in a special election in January 1932 and hence became the first woman elected to the U.S. Senate.

On May 9, 1932, she became the first woman to preside over the Senate while Vice President Charles Curtis was on rest and relaxation break. At this point, she announced her intention to run for reelection. This came as a shock to many who failed to understand the depth of her newfound ambitions. Hattie Caraway was indeed reelected in 1932 after campaigning with Huey P. Long of Louisiana.

In 1938, she ran again for reelection against Congressman John McClellan. McClellan came up with the snarky and sexist campaign slogan of: "We need another man in the Senate." But while McClellan tried to minimize the little lady, she created a genuine political strategy by rallying the support of veterans and union workers. She soundly defeated McClellan. After years of Arkansas politicking, Caraway was defeated by J. William Fulbright in 1944.

Her Senate legacy includes the nickname "Silent Hattie," as she spoke on the floor so rarely. She was a tireless worker for the Equal Nationality Treaty of 1934. The treaty gave woman many nationality rights that had been previously limited to only men. And in 1943, she became the first woman in the Senate to sponsor what would become known as the Equal Rights Amendment. Hattie had a stroke and died in 1950. She is buried in Oaklawn Cemetery in Jonesboro. One of the town's main streets is named for her. Nice job, Senator!

HAZEL LEONA WALKER: ARKANSAS'S FIRST LADY OF BASKETBALL

Hazel Walker was born on August 6, 1914, on the family farm in Oak Hill. She was the only daughter of Herbert and Minnie Walker. The Walkers were Arkansas natives of Cherokee descent. Hazel would become one of the great legends of the sport of basketball.

Hazel hit the boards for the first time in 1928 as a freshman at Ashdown High School as part of the Pantherettes. By her senior year, she had been named an All-Conference star three times and All-District twice and grew into an impressive physical specimen—a fact not lost on her teammates, males in general and the fans who watched from the stands.

In fact, Hazel Walker scored the title of "Most Beautiful Girl in the Tournament" when the Pantherettes went to Little Rock for the first-ever girls' state high school basketball tournament. The year was 1932.

After graduation, she was given a scholarship to play for an unlikely team known as the Tulsa Business College

Stenographers. Even playing for a team with a horrible and uninspiring name, Hazel was a solid winner. She won the 1934 AAU national championship, and that won her a place on an All-American team. She also won the hearts of the crowds who watched her play.

Years of victories, team transitions, awards, titles, praise and the tragic loss of her husband led to Hazel's decision to turn professional. In 1946, she joined the All-American Red Heads. The Red Heads toured the country and competed mostly against men's teams made of local leaders and celebrities in an entertainment-based spectacle something akin to the Harlem Globetrotters.

Hazel eventually tired of being a gender-based novelty act and formed her own team in 1949, called Hazel Walker's Arkansas Travelers.

In a sharp departure from the Red Heads, the Travelers sought no entertainment advantage in the game. They played basketball, and they played it straight and hard. In fact, they played over two hundred games a season, more than three times the NBA schedule of the day. And, oh yeah, they pretty much mopped the court with all the men's teams they competed against. On average, they won 85 percent of their games.

To keep things fun, Hazel developed a half-time event that helped drive the success of her team financially. Hazel would walk to the center of the court and challenge all comers to a free-throw competition. Free throws from half court, kneeling, sitting, over the head, behind the back, every trick shot in the book—you name it—Hazel would attempt it. In over 3,500 challenges, Hazel reigned supreme!

In 1965, she retired after sixteen record-breaking, precedent-setting seasons with the Travelers. The next year, she was inducted in the Helm's Women's Amateur Basketball Hall of Fame in Los Angeles. Hazel enjoyed hunting and fishing and relaxing in America's Natural State until her death in 1990. What a gal!

NORTHEAST ARKANSAS'S HERO OF FAITH: MORRIS BERGER

Earlier in this book, we told you the forgotten tale of the Jonesboro Church War of 1931. After presenting this story for over three years on our Jonesboro Ghost Tour, we made a fascinating discovery. We caught a glimpse of the external factors that may have fueled the insanity of such anger and violence on the part of the townspeople. As it turns out, in December 1931, which was the height of the church war, northeast Arkansas was feeling the pain of the Depression.

The poverty rate was soaring in an area already characterized by low wages and tough working conditions. Foreclosures on homes reached an all-time high, and children were hitting the roads in search of anything better anywhere else.

We have come to believe that this drove much of the outrageous behavior, especially the anger expressed toward elected officials and political leaders. In many ways, it was a time similar to the one we live in today. Only worse! Very few people in Jonesboro are aware of the town's history. Even fewer know that the town nearly fell apart at the end of 1931. And none, it seems, know of the faithful man who saved the town. This is his story.

Morris Berger came to Arkansas as an Austrian immigrant in 1881. He was determined to make his way and succeed in America. He was also a very devout Jewish man.

Morris began as a cart merchant. He pushed his cart of goods from door-to-door and sold various odds and ends to everyone. In time, his enterprise grew to include the first furniture company in northeast Arkansas and the first real grocery, textiles and dry goods stores.

Over the years, Mr. Berger became a leading businessman and a powerful and wealthy player in Jonesboro. Mr. Berger's hard work and faith led him to help establish a Jewish synagogue in Jonesboro, as well as a Jewish cemetery. He built his house at 1120 South Main Street, where it still stands today. The Berger House is on the National Register of Historic Places and even served as the public library for Jonesboro from the late 1940s to the mid-1960s.

This is the beautiful historic home of Morris Berger in Jonesboro. It has also been a law office, a carpet store and the county library. *Photo by Heather Stanley.*

Back at the end of 1931, while the fundamentalist Christians were being held at bay from killing one another by martial law and federal troops, Mr. Berger was seeing the impact of the Great Depression on his town, the town to which he felt so grateful for his success.

By December 11, all five banks in Jonesboro, Arkansas, had collapsed. The town had no financial means to sustain itself. Jonesboro, Arkansas, was in a money crisis. Mr. Berger responded quickly and boldly. He called his sons back to Jonesboro for a family meeting. Together, they made decisions that literally saved the town. On January 6, 1932, funded by Berger family money, Mercantile Bank opened on Main Street.

The full-page newspaper ad announced that funds were available and that all were welcome to come to the bank to discuss their needs and business matters. Mercantile Bank became the backbone that both sustained and grew Jonesboro into the future. This act of generosity would give Jonesboro a happy ending.

But there would be no happy ending for Mr. Berger. By February, he was feeling the sting of loss on his own businesses, and with most of his cash placed in Mercantile Bank to save the town, his personal wealth was failing. So despondent was he over this that he became depressed. He felt like a failure and quietly slipped into despair.

In the dark of night on February 3, he acted on desperate plans. He sent his family away for the evening, and while they were gone, he wrote letters to his loved ones, laid out his papers and affairs on his long dining room table and ingested a large dose of mercury bichloride. This is an extremely powerful acidic poison used as an industrial disinfectant.

Morris Berger then called and asked the telephone operator to summon his family to come back to his home. They did, but of course it was too late to reverse the effects of the acid. He was transported to the hospital but died as his internal organs were literally dissolved from the inside out. It was a grisly end for a man who had proven himself so noble.

It is a study in sharp contrasts to compare the outrageous behavior of a large part of the Christian population fighting and warring with one another over whose evangelist was the best while this quiet man of faith literally gave himself to save their town. The bigger mystery here is how this man has become such a forgotten tale of Arkansas. God bless you, Mr. Berger. We won't forget you!

10

Forbidden Fruit

Ah, behold the wonder that is the Osage apple! This remarkable product of nature is a familiar sight in the Natural State. It is that ridiculous green-yellow, bumpy, softball-sized thing that fills the streets and yards of your neighborhood. It will also leave a memorable dent embedded in your car if you are unfortunate enough to park below one that decides to attack.

It looks like a kind of failed experiment to cross breed a grapefruit with a cauliflower and a pinecone. If you've ever seen one, you have no doubt had the natural inclination to kick the thing. If you followed that urge, you likely made another discovery. It holds a storehouse of strange white milky sap within its goofy looking exterior. This little freak of nature comes from the Bodark tree.

The name Bodark comes from slurring the French words *bois d'arc*. That may sound like the name of a promising new lager beer but is in fact the term for "wood of the bow." It is believed that term originated with the Osage Indians, who used this type of wood in making bows. More importantly, the term *bois d'arc* may be the origin of our word for Ozark.

In addition to providing a weird-looking conversation piece, we know that the apple has properties that serve as a natural mosquito repellant. Now that is a useful trait in Arkansas!

Squirrels, opossums and horses have been known to eat the apples, although they can pose a very real choking hazard. Some researchers now link the disappearance of certain extinct animals to a love of the apple. Topping the list of critters that were done in by the hedge apple is the mastodon. You would have to admit, the hedge apple does look like a mastodon snack.

And in Arkansas, all history will no doubt find a way to link to some sort of Bible-related lesson. So here it is—the official folklore version of the Bodark tree and its freaky fruit.

The story is told that the Bodark tree gave the most beautiful, delicious and nutritious fruit known to man. In fact, the Bodark was the tree in the center of the Garden of Eden. It was man using the fruit in his original sin that caused God to turn the fruit into a hideous, ugly, mostly useless thing. This also explains why the wood of the tree has been used in the making of so many weapons of destruction.

THE ARKANSAS BLACK APPLE

The skin of this fancy fruit ranges in color from dark red to black. It is a true native apple that only grows naturally in the Ozarks. It is a variation of a Winesap apple, which was first produced in 1870 by a Mr. Brathwaite of Bentonville.

This tasty dark treat accounts for up to 5 percent of Arkansas's apple crop and is most commonly used in cobblers and other cooked dishes.

THE FARKLEBERRY

The tree species *Vaccinium arboretum* of the family Ericaceous is also known as the sparkleberry. But in Arkansas, it is known as the farkleberry. It is a small black berry that makes fine eating for birds but not humans.

The farkleberry maintains notoriety in the Natural State only for its association with former governor Orval Faubus. Governor Faubus and this ignoble berry bush were lampooned in a series of cartoons created by George Edward Fisher.

It seems that Faubus put on a pair of dirty overalls and took up an axe for a photo opportunity with road workers in Franklin County. The governor made a great show of directing the actions of the workers as they cleared brush and weeds. He then took the press on a tour along the road as he correctly identified the more valuable trees, including dogwoods and redbuds, that he insisted be left for natural beauty.

The staged, rehearsed nature of this event was not lost on the press. In fact, knowing they were simply being used to make the governor look like a good-hearted, outdoorsy, conservation-minded individual brought out the mischievous side of at least one reporter.

The Arkansas Parks and Tourism Commission published the photos and an article that listed the trees Faubus named and singled out for salvation. Our Mr.

The Blue Springs Heritage Center in Eureka Springs allows visitors to get very close to the amazing blue spring. This spring bursts forth and gushes millions of gallons of water a day. *Photo by Heather Stanley.*

Fisher made the editorial decision to drop the useless farkleberry tree into the list.

After that, the term farkleberry and Faubus were synonymous. Faubus was enraged by the prank until he realized that embracing the joke made him seem more human and humble. So he used it to his own advantage. He started calling the walking path behind his home his "farkleberry trail."

In 1967, *The Farkleberry Follies* came to life courtesy of the Arkansas Chapter of the Society of Professional Journalists. The stage show featured broad political satires, as well as regional celebrities, to raise money for journalism scholarships.

Mr. Fisher's now legendary cartoons found a permanent home on the walls of the Farkleberry Restaurant in the Regions Bank in Little Rock.

11

The Tantrabobus Will Get You If You Don't Watch Out!

G hosts, monsters and haunted people, places and things have always been part of the human experience. It turns out there is a useful purpose for our ghosts and the stories in which they live. Arkansas history is full of strange and mysterious incidents; consequently, Arkansas culture is filled with a rich tradition of various superstitions and folklore designed to guide a faithful soul through the mine field that is life itself.

The Tantrabobus

The Tantrabobus is the name given by Ozark hill folk to any needed monster or devil creature. I say needed because the most familiar story associated with the Tantrabobus is that of a well monster. And by that, I mean a monster that lives deep down in your water well.

Children would be brought up on the tale that they should never lean over and look down into the well. They were told that doing so would incur the wrath of a horrible beast that would jump up, grab them, pull them into the well and devour them. That's a very scary thing if you're a kid. Or an adult, for that matter!

Truth is, the well monster story is at least as practical as it is scary. Children in those rural areas had to be taught not to lean over the opening of the well or they might indeed perish—not from the Tantrabobus but from falling into the well with no help in sight.

So herein is an example of how monsters (and ghosts) are used to teach cautionary tales for the preservation of the species. It almost makes you want to watch M. Night Shyamalan's *The Village* a second time. Well, almost.

Now for those of you who "ain't from around here," the good news is that the Tantrabobus is still part of your world. As it turns out, the word "Tantrabobus" has been shortened, slurred and altered into "that boogey," as in boogeyman, as well as the even shorter word "bogus." So if you know that your boogeyman is bogus, you should thank your Tantrabobus twice.

THE BURNING BRIDE

The good book tells us in Corinthians 7:9 that "it is better to marry than to burn." The verse refers to marriage as a proper outlet for sexual energies. Every moral tenant has a bushel batch of related folklore attached to help get the point across to the next generation. One of the most familiar of these tales is that of "The Burning Bride."

The story goes that a sweet young lady is preparing for her wedding night and is twirling about in her wedding dress. At some unfortunate point, the dress brushes the sparks of the fireplace, and in a moment's time, she is engulfed in flames. Terrified, she runs into the woods but cannot escape her fiery fate.

Legend holds that to this day you can see the flickering light of flames dashing wildly to and fro in those same woods where the bride is eternally burning, trapped between this world and the next.

This little tale of terror is another cautionary tale designed to reinforce the cultural mentality that when we get too happy or too full of ourselves, disaster and judgment will soon follow. This is why ambition, individuality and pleasure are always connected to some sort of emotional red flag. These ingrained values have played a major role in shaping the progress (and lack of it) in Arkansas.

THE CRESCENT HOTEL GHOSTS

Reportedly the most haunted hotel in America, the Crescent Hotel in Eureka Springs, Arkansas, sits magnificently perched atop the artist colony turned tourist town. The

Crescent has some standing ghost residents who appear with some regularity and are known by name to some of the locals and hotel employees. There is Michael, a man who allegedly died during the construction of the hotel.

A lady ghost named Theodora is believed to haunt room 419. She is probably friends with the ghosts that reportedly haunt rooms 218 and 414. Another ghost seen is an elegant, bearded man in formal dress clothes who frequents the lobby and bar of the hotel.

Rocking chairs on the back porch rock by themselves, and visitors' luggage repacks itself and blocks the doors. All

The legendary Crescent Hotel. Many claim it is the most haunted hotel in America. *Photo by Heather Stanley.*

manner of mysterious mischief is attributed to these restless spirits. But why are they here? Where did they come from?

The root of the hundreds of ghostly tales, photos, ghost tours and one of the more stunning episodes of TV's *The Ghost Hunters* is a very unusual man: Mr. Norman Baker. He was known during his days as owner of the Crescent as Dr. Norman Baker.

Dr. Baker bought the hotel and turned it into a hospital and health center in 1937. But sadly for the thousands of patients who would soon flock to the Crescent for help and hope, Mr. Norman never attended medical school and had no medical training whatsoever. It all came down to the fact that he considered himself a healthcare professional.

He believed that he invented dozens of cures for everything from headaches to cancer. He also held the conviction that the AMA, and others in organized medicine, did not want him to share his wonderful cures with the world and that his enemies were out to kill him. So Dr. Baker retrofitted the vintage hotel to include hidden tunnels behind secret doors where machine guns were hung at the ready in case jealous legitimate healthcare professionals tried to attack and capture him.

As for his cures, they mostly consisted of drinking and bathing in the legendary healing waters of Eureka Springs, along with some oddball home remedy rituals. One of the cures for brain cancer was to pull back the scalp, flood the affected area with spring water and embed watermelon seeds against the growth.

Even though the good doctor was eventually brought up on criminal charges for mail fraud, the official stories say no one died at the Crescent. However, local lore tells a much darker tale.

The inside story is that Dr. Baker was a rather monstrous figure who experimented on patients with horrific and absurd treatments. When persons died under his care, their bodies were burned in the furnace or disposed of via the basement autopsy table and sink. Dozens of skeletons and skulls have been found, as well as jars of preserved human body parts and organ over the years, secreted within the walls and around the basement morgue area.

Proof that you can't believe everything you read. *Photo by Allen Fromars.*

Dr. Baker covered up the demise of his patients and continued to collect the families' payments to his institution until the hospital closed in 1940, when he was arrested by federal authorities. The fact that the Crescent is said to be haunted underscores one of the most important lessons we can learn from our ghost stories.

Ghosts reveal a just universe. This reinforces our most treasured spiritual beliefs. The value of the individual coupled with eternal justice that reaches beyond the grave are benchmarks of our hauntings. The patients of the hospital were wronged, and the ghost stories give them

One single rocking chair out of a line continued to rock by itself, stopped when touched and then resumed again. Is it haunted by Dr. Baker or was he just off his rocker? *Photo by Edward Underwood.*

a way to be heard and the wrong noted. Meanwhile, Dr. Baker himself haunts the hotel out of regret.

So the sociological value of the ghost story is to remind us that dirty deeds don't go unpunished and injustice will be avenged. This may be the single most powerful reason that every culture on earth has and keeps its ghost stories generation after generation.

By the way, there are nightly ghost tours of the Crescent and Basin Park Hotels in Eureka Springs. And yes, you get to walk through the morgue, and yes, local psychics will affirm and indentify the various spirits for you. They also encourage you to take lots of pictures—especially pictures in the hotel's mirrors. You never know what, or who, you might see in them.

12

Very Superstitious

Did you know that Winston Churchill was afraid of Fridays? He carried a lucky walking stick on Fridays and refused to travel at all on a Friday the Thirteenth. Hard to believe he is the bold leader who said, "We have nothing to fear but fear itself." Cornelius Vanderbilt had his bed legs resting in four bowls of salt to ward off evil spirits. President Harry Truman insisted on nailing a horseshoe over the door of his White House office.

Cuba Gooding Jr. carries a secret good luck charm at all times. He claims that if he reveals it to anyone, it won't work anymore. We can only imagine he showed it to someone about the time he made *Snow Dogs*. Jennifer Anniston won't board an airplane unless her right foot goes in first and she can tap on the outside of the plane. Tiger Woods claimed red was his lucky color. Of course, that was a few years ago.

Much like ghosts, monsters and haunts, our Arkansas history is filled with superstitions. The breeding ground for such apparently irrational thought and practice seems to be the need to interact with the unknown. In the vast vacuum of the unknowable, our minds strive to create a path of ritual or practice that will allow us to influence the outcome of things in our favor.

Arkansas is filled with mystical beliefs that are an odd mix of various aspects of mainstream religious traditions. Anthropologists suggest that "religion appears when magic has failed" or "magic appears when religion has failed." What seems obvious is that as long as people have been filled with uncertainty, there have been superstitions to fill the gaps. Here are a few choice items.

The Bible–New American Superstition Edition

Many Arkansans seem to believe not so much the words in the Bible but the idea that the Bible itself carries supernatural blessings and abilities. Bible superstitions include using a Bible as a protective shield. Some soldiers carry small Bibles for this reason. A Bible under a pillow or next to a baby's bed is a common practice to bring protection.

Apparently, the good book is not only a defense but an offense, too. A single, well-chosen page from a Bible placed under a doormat will make robbers stumble and fail.

Reciting any verse from the Bible three times with an enemy's name between each repetition will bring down a horrible curse on that individual. Other beliefs included methods of using the Bible to divine the future. A large key suspended from a cord can be used like a pendulum over an open Bible to point to a passage that will give important direction or answer questions.

And should the aforementioned practice of using a Bible page under the doormat not stop the robbers, a cord can be run through a key, the Bible closed and tied shut around the key and then hung from a nail in the ceiling. The Bible will turn to point at any guilty party in the room. This is much faster than the court system.

Another practice known as bibliomancy is very common in variant forms all over the world. Quite simply, a prayer for an answer is offered, and the book is allowed to fall open to a random page. Study of the page will reveal the answer that was sought.

GETTING CROSS OVER RELIGION

The use of a cross symbol dates to ancient Scandinavians, who used crosses to mark property lines and put them over the graves of leaders. Egyptians used the cross as a sacred symbol as well.

In the modern world, the cross is most closely associated with Christianity but is also a common symbol in many superstitions. It is believed to ward off evil. It is not necessary to use an actual physical cross to gain its benefits. Crossing the fingers or legs is enough. Any food marked with a cross, like hot cross buns, is considered protected from evil spirits. From now on, I am going to squeeze out a ketchup cross on the top of every double cheeseburger I order.

MIRROR, MIRROR OFF THE WALL

In Arkansas, the first mirrors were actually the surface of any available standing water. Staring at your reflection could be done to determine your future, but don't overdo it. This practice comes with the warning that you might go insane.

The logic for this was the belief that when you gazed at your image, you were seeing your soul. This idea continued forward to the innovation of glass mirrors.

Many years ago, it was believed that if your mirror broke, an unspeakable disaster would come down on you. Today, this has been rolled back to a simple seven-year stretch of bad luck.

Since mirrors could be used to tell the future, when a mirror falls off a wall and breaks, it was believed that God was preventing the owner from seeing some unfortunate upcoming event. It was strictly forbidden to show a baby its own reflection before one year of age. If the baby saw itself before that point, it would die very young.

In the Ozarks, many still cover mirrors at night. This ensures that their souls will not wander into the mirror

A creepy stonework owl carved into the fireplace at the Crescent Hotel. *Photo by Karen Underwood.*

and become trapped there forever. One of the most overtly occult mirror superstitions is the practice of scrying. This was the divination method of choice for none other than Nostradamus. The scryer gazes into the reflective surface until reaching a trance-like state in which visions of the future are seen.

PICTURE IMPERFECT

Much like mirrors, pictures can also possess the soul of the subject. I use this superstition in my live show during a ghost story sequence.

It was also believed that if your picture fell from the wall for no apparent reason, you would soon die.

A curse can be placed on someone by turning his picture to the wall or hanging it upside down. Who knew the cosmic forces of the universe could be manipulated by such seemingly innocent gestures?

Noting the Time of Death

A more contemporary country superstition is that a person's clock will stop ticking at the precise moment of their death. There are many supposed incidents of this clock/death time mystery. Some clocks that belonged to famous persons are left stopped as a memorial to the deceased.

It is also held by some Arkansans that a clock striking more than twelve times is signaling that someone within earshot will soon pass on. Really soon—before the next time the clock strikes.

It's worth pointing out that older clocks required a lot of attention from their owners in terms of winding them up each day. Consequently, if the owner fell ill or didn't tend to daily chores, his clock would soon stop. Although that makes sense, I'm sure that the angel of death himself stops the clock as a creepy omen. I'm pretty sure, anyway.

LITTLE COUNTRY CHURCH

Superstitions about churches are usually always about gaining protection from evil in most any form. Almost anything in or from the church can be a good luck charm.

Oddly, meeting a clergyman unexpectedly is considered very bad luck, as they are associated with sad occasions like funerals. If a bird lands on the weather vane of the church, a death will soon happen. If the church door rattles unexpectedly, a death will soon happen.

And if you sit inside the church from 11:00 p.m. until midnight on Halloween, you will see the ghostly manifestations of all church members who will die in the coming year. In other words, it's just like a business committee meeting at most churches.

GRAVE ISSUES

Graves were traditionally positioned so the deceased had their feet facing east and heads pointing west. That way, on judgment day, they could rise up and walk eastward easily. Now, that's just good thinking. If you walk over the grave of an unbaptized person, you could die of "gravemerelles." Sounds like everyone needs to be baptized!

Placing wreaths on graves started as magic circles to keep the deceased's ghost from leaving the coffin. In the old days, people were encouraged to draw or place a circle

Thorncrown Chapel, a magnificent glass structure surrounded by nature, is a favorite place for Arkansas weddings and other special occasions. *Photo by Heather Stanley.*

on a grave to ensure that the person's ghost would not rise from the ground and haunt the living. This is the origin of putting floral wreaths on graves. So you see, we aren't superstitious anymore, but why take chances?

13

Life, Liberty and the Pursuit of Unhappiness

Arkansas has an ongoing battle with its Confederate past. Many still cling to the trappings of the pre–*Gone With the Wind* ideal of the South. Some are just plain bigots. Herein is a story from the past that lays bare the mindset of the old South and one determined individual who tried to break free.

Mr. Hackett is believed to have been born in the year 1810. It would be a year that Nelson would come to both celebrate and regret. His personal journey is representative of those of countless slaves during this time in Arkansas history. The level of cruelty and persecution exceeds belief.

Some thirty years of life passed without notice, but in June 1840, Mr. Hackett was sold to Alfred Wallace. Mr. Wallace was a very wealthy plantation owner, retailer and land speculator in Washington County.

The records reveal that Nelson Hackett was described as a "Negro dandy" of about thirty years of age. Consequently, he was assigned the task of being Mr. Wallace's personal valet and butler.

In mid-July 1841, Nelson ran away from Wallace, taking with him a coat, a saddle, a gold watch and Wallace's fastest horse. He was headed for Canada. Six wild weeks later, he arrived in the Great White North. No doubt hungry, he finally came to rest in the town of Sandwich, south of Ontario.

And of course, Wallace was in hot pursuit, along with his associate George C. Grigg. Nelson's path was discovered, and depositions were given that led to his arrest and incarceration in Sandwich. Nelson confessed to the crimes but later said that he had been beaten during his interrogation.

By September, Wallace and Grigg had made it to Michigan to begin extradition proceedings against Nelson. Michigan's acting governor, J. Wright Gordon, issued a formal request to the Canadian government for Nelson to be turned over to U.S. authorities.

William Henry Draper, attorney general for Upper Canada, refused. He pointed out that the state of original jurisdiction, Arkansas, hadn't made the request. Therefore, Wallace and Grigg returned to Arkansas, pressing criminal charges in Fayetteville.

On November 26, 1841, a grand jury indicted Hackett for grand larceny. Arkansas governor Archibald Yell, a friend of Mr. Wallace, made a formal request to Canadian authorities for Nelson's extradition four days later.

Nelson Hackett begged to be allowed to stay in Canada. He argued that in Arkansas he would be "tortured in a manner that to hang him at once would be a mercy."

However, in mid-January 1842, Canadian authorities ordered that Nelson be extradited. On February 7, 1842, Nelson Hackett found himself bound and gagged and transported across the border.

Nelson spent two months in solitary confinement in a Detroit jail, while his captors waited for the winter weather to clear and allow further travel. Detroit abolitionists initially hoped to use his case in their campaign against slavery, but Nelson's theft of Wallace's property complicated the matter.

That spring, Onesimus Evans and Lewis Davenport, who were responsible for transporting Nelson back to Arkansas, brought Nelson to Chicago and boarded a stagecoach for Peoria, Illinois. On May 21, 1842, during a stopover in Princeton, Illinois, Nelson escaped once more. Unfortunately, he was caught two days later.

On May 26, he was locked up in Missouri, and by June, he was back in Fayetteville.

Nelson's case led to much public outcry in Canada. In fact, the *Canadian Western Herald* stated that legal fees incurred by Wallace amounted to $1,500, much more than Nelson's market value as a slave.

Returning Nelson Hackett to his owner was counter to Canadian traditions regarding fugitive slaves. Previous extradition laws had never mentioned escaped slaves. Likely as a result of the Hackett case, Article 10 of the Webster-

Ashburton Treaty, approved by the British and American governments on August 9, 1842, restricted extradition to criminals, thereby protecting fugitive slaves.

Nothing certain is known about Nelson's fate. He never went to trial on the charges that led to his extradition. Another slave who escaped from Wallace allegedly said that Nelson was bound, tortured and whipped repeatedly in front of all the slaves. Nelson may have been sold to someone in Texas. British abolitionists tried to purchase and free him, but no trace of the transaction or his whereabouts could be found. Hatred is not easily appeased. God rest ye, Nelson.

It is interesting to note that in the New Testament Book of Philemon, the main character is a runaway slave named Onesimus. The slave owner is implored to receive his runaway back with kindness. Perhaps more time reading a Bible and less time waving one would be useful.

14

Samuel Peel and His Big Teepee

Sam Peel was born in Independence County on September 13, 1831. Peel distinguished himself from an early age by hard work and fierce independence coupled with great ambition.

He worked as both a clerk in his father's store and as deputy court clerk to his father. Peel became enamored of the affections of the affluent Mary Emaline Berry. Miss Berry refused Peel's rather forward requests for her hand in marriage until he promised her a grand palace of a house as a wedding gift.

This began the construction of what is now known as the Peel Mansion. The house stands its proud ground in Bentonville, Arkansas. It is a tourist attraction, a popular place for social events and private parties and a source of historic education for visitors and students.

The Peel Mansion has become a tourist attraction since its renovation. The project was underwritten by Walmart. *Photo by Edward Underwood.*

The home of this lawyer-scholar-businessman-warrior is currently sitting on the edge of a Walmart parking lot. Well, it is in Bentonville after all. In fact, Walmart is the main sponsor of the house exhibit and underwrote most of its renovation and restoration. Peel himself is most famous for becoming the first native-born Arkansan to be elected to the U.S. Congress.

His role in Congress led him to accept the House chairmanship of the Committee on Indian Affairs. As such, he was charged with managing the education and care of Indians and their lands. He also had to negotiate

Above: Samuel Peel's house was called the "Big Teepee" by the representatives of the Native American tribes with whom he negotiated land and labor treaties. *Photo by Karen Underwood.*

Left: A fashionable street sign in the downtown square of Bentonville. Crystal Bridges is a wonderful museum sponsored by Walmart, and the Peel Mansion is too. The library is just a block up from the Walmart Visitors' Center. *Photo by Edward Underwood.*

This storefront in the Bentonville town square was the location of the original store Sam Walton had prior to launching the Walmart revolution. Locals joke about how long it will be before the town is called Waltonville. *Photo by Edward Underwood.*

land deals and land payments to the Indians in exchange for creating roads and other bits of creative usage.

Many of these meetings were held on Peel's front yard. The teepees would be pitched and the Indians invited inside the mansion to settle claims. The Indians came to refer to the Peel Mansion as the "Big Teepee." Once inside the Big Teepee, the Indians were paid for treaty agreements. By the end of his career, Peel specialized in providing legal advice to Indians and was appointed the official attorney for all civilized tribes.

The Peel Mansion offers visitors a chance to see how wealthy and powerful men lived in the late 1800s. It is beautifully restored, has a gift shop and a magnificent garden showcase and, oh yeah, is very close to a Walmart.

15

The Bridgeford House

Captain John Bridgeford was a man of action, a man of honor, a man of means and, perhaps, a man of mystery.

John Bridgeford made a name for himself serving the Confederacy during the Civil War. Most notably, he was a part of the action at the legendary Battle of Pea Ridge. Once the war was over, the captain retired, and he and his wife, Mary, built their now famous house on Spring Street in Eureka Springs, Arkansas. It was 1884 when their grand "painted lady" house was completed.

The Bridgefords ran the Pence House hotel on Main Street until it burned down in one of the many epic fires that purged Eureka Springs in those postwar years. But it was the Bridgefords' personal home that was the envy of the neighbors. It was extravagant, with every aspect of its construction being completed with the best materials and best labor available. Many wondered how a retired

Confederate captain turned hotel manager could afford such a home. This is where our mysteries begin.

It has long been rumored that certain Confederate officers made creative use of some of the army's payroll and other resources. It seems that once the Confederate loss was more or less inevitable, these abuses become common, as the men began thinking about what would face them after the war. If you remember our earlier chapter about Albert Pike, a man who led troops at Pea Ridge, he was also accused of creative dispersion of army resources.

There are two theories about these kinds of war stories. One is that manipulative men took advantage of a situation to further themselves at the expense of the Confederate army. Another is that Confederate advocates spread these stories to help rationalize their loss of the war. I would like to suggest a third scenario. I believe it is a combination of both. Profiteering from war is as American as stolen apple pie.

In the case of Captain Bridgeford, there are two pieces of evidence that may suggest he directed some "loose change" into his own pocket. First, the home he built probably was much more than a retired army captain and hotel manager could afford. The second evidence is Captain Bridgeford's mysterious tunnel that comes up next to his expensive house.

One of the popular stories of wartime is that a network of tunnels was created around the area to provide getaways for any number of occasions. Perhaps a military officer

Captain John Bridgeford built this lovely home for him and his wife. Just how the captain afforded such elegance is the subject of historical debate. *Photo by Edward Underwood.*

could escape capture by running into a secret tunnel. Other stories around Eureka Springs indicate that such tunnels also led from the post office and city offices to the "body house" and beyond.

The rumor around Captain John Bridgeford is that one such tunnel was created leading up to the building site of his home and that this tunnel was stashed with the cash from the army. This would be the money that Bridgeford would access to pay for the construction and other luxuries.

No one can be sure if these stories are true or if they are merely whispers from a jealous past. The Bridgeford House

Jeff and Sam Feldman are the current owners of the Bridgeford House. *Photo by Edward Underwood.*

itself is amazing. Today, it is part of the largest downtown entry into the National Register of Historic Places and is a very popular five-room bed-and-breakfast.

The current owners of the Bridgeford House are Jeff and Sam Feldman. The Feldmans regularly welcome visitors from all over the world into the historic house for both long and short-term vacation.

Over the years of living in and taking care of the Bridgeford House, Jeff told me he believes the house still holds some secrets. Last summer, while having some work done on the home, a tattered copy of the New Testament literally fell from the walls. It was dated 1869. The workers deduced that over the decades the book must have fallen through the attic rafters into a wall and finally escaped during the work inside that wall. Who knows what story that old Bible could tell?

But what of the fabled tunnel of Mr. Bridgeford's secreted wealth? Jeff believes he has found it. On the side of the support wall where there is now a decorative metal wheel and some beautiful plants, you can see a change in the pattern of the bricking—a large round area that clearly appears different from the surrounding edge. Could this be the bricked-up entrance to his money tunnel?

The change in bricking and discoloration may be a clue to the reality of Captain Bridgeford's alleged hidden tunnel. *Photo courtesy of Jeff Feldman.*

The Feldmans have noticed that the area on the wall under the entrance steps to the house and around the edge of the newer bricking does not frost in the winter in the same pattern as the rest of the surfaces. Would an excavation of that mysterious area on the wall reveal a Civil War secret? For the moment, no one knows for certain, but it is a fascinating possibility that would line up with a grand bit of folklore.

Another side of this forgotten tale is that when Mr. Bridgeford died, he had not shared the secret of his money stash with his beloved wife, Mary. This left the widow Bridgeford to fend for herself without the benefit of the previously available resources.

Times grew very hard for Mary, and her time in their magnificent house ended in strife and hardship. Some believe that Mary Bridgeford haunts the house, still looking for her husband and his help. Of the haunting, Jeff Feldman tells me that ghost hunters have visited the house and report that Mary is, in fact, present. Jeff has experienced some odd circumstances and happenings in the home, including his CD player being repeatedly shut off with no one else in the room.

The Bridgeford House B&B's official pet, Sophie, a socially gregarious miniature Schnauzer, has been known to bark at no one in the stairwell on many occasions. None of these ghostly goings-on seem to dampen anyone's spirits when having a good time as a guest in the beautiful house. People continue to enjoy and benefit from Captain

Sophie, the Bridgeford's house dog, welcomes guests and makes everyone feel at home. *Photo by Karen Underwood.*

Bridgeford's home, and as for the stories, secret tunnels, money and ghosts? For now, they remain another mystery on Spring Street. If you want to investigate this historic location for yourself, you can book a stay at www. bridgefordhouse.com.

16

THE GREATEST NEARLY ACADEMIC FRAUD IN ARKANSAS HISTORY

Hey, have you heard the one about the acid-tongued New York reporter, the Little Rock crusader and the deaf metal smith from Jonesboro? No? Well, take a deep breath, and we shall recount for you a twisted tale of egos, relics, culture wars and the mysterious head of King Crowley.

In 1920, one of the most popular newspapermen in New York City was the legendary H.L. Mencken. Mencken was the prototype of the hard-living, hard-nosed, critical big city reporter. He spoke with reckless abandon on all topics at all times. This made him a sensation. It also made him a much-hated man by those on the receiving end of his sharp-witted attacks.

It was in that very year that Mencken wrote an article called "The Sahara of the Bozarks." This article tore into the southern states with cynical glee. While he painted the entire South as being backward and superstitious,

Arkansas received more than its fair share of stinging rebukes.

In his article, he pointed out that in all the wasteland that is Arkansas, there was not a single art gallery showing any notable works, no theaters devoted to worthwhile plays, no philosophers or theologians thriving. He called Arkansas "the apex of moronia." And as far as visible signs of culture and heritage, he was pretty much right.

In 1925, Mencken's written attacks inspired Anita Loos to write the bestselling novel *Gentlemen Prefer Blondes*. She creates the main character, Lorelei Lee, as a low-intellect product of the best breeding that Little Rock could offer. The success of the novel and Mencken's continued jabs only furthered the stereotype of Arkansas that took root from the time of "Lum and Abner."

Now, all this negative attention raised the ire of one industrious woman. Julia Burnelle Smade Babcock, nicknamed "Bernie," was an Arkansas native who had spent time in New York learning her craft as a writer and poet. She was working for the fledgling *Arkansas Democrat* newspaper as society page editor.

Interestingly enough, Bernie claims it was a passionate article she read as a child that made her want to become a writer. The article was in a leaflet passed out by the Women's Temperance Christian Union in 1884. The WTCU at that time was partnering with Carry A. Nation.

Bernie decided to take matters into her own hands and show those northern cynics all the worthwhile art, culture and history that Arkansas did have. She decided to raise the money and open a Museum of Discovery right on Main Street in Little Rock. This would put Arkansas on the map and show its past and future as bright, thriving and growing.

She found herself with plenty of advocates and supporters, and with the building secured, she sent out letters and advertisements for exhibits and collections to be displayed. She also lobbed her own editorial barbs back at H.L. Mencken. This proved unwise. Entering into a war of words with Mencken was one of those things that simply should not be done. Like starting a land war in Russia during the winter.

But Bernie was certain she would have the final word when her museum revealed to the public a grand and important archaeological discovery that had recently been unearthed. It seems a man named Dentler Rowland, a deaf gunsmith, metal worker and jeweler from Jonesboro, Arkansas, had contacted her with an amazing story.

Mr. Rowland described to Miss Babcock how he literally stumbled across ancient artifacts on his land at Crowley's Ridge. Digging up the protrusions that stumbled him, he said he uncovered a stash of stone figurines, busts and items that looked very "museumy" to him. In fact, he said the pieces looked very ancient and like Egyptian or Aztec drawings he had seen in books. He suggested that the pieces might belong to a lost

In 1927, Mrs. Bernie Babcock, a founding director of the Natural History Museum in Little Rock, purchased a portion of the collection, paying Dentler Rowland $500, a lot of money at the time. For years Mrs. Babcock promoted the collection as genuine and attempted from time to time to authenticate them as prehistoric artifacts.

These are letters from Dentler Rowland to Bernie Babcock between 1927 and 1928.

The first page of literal transcriptions of communication between Bernie Babcock and Dentler Rowland over his questionable archaeological discovery from the ASU Museum archives. *Photo by Heather Stanley.*

civilization. Mr. Rowland had recently become aware of Miss Babcock's museum and its quest for notable exhibits. He asked if the museum would be interested in buying the artifacts from him.

Well, the idea that ancient Egyptians or Aztecs had once chosen Arkansas as their home and that they left behind history, art and culture generated immediate excitement and pride. Miss Babcock's investor group quickly communicated with Rowland that it would love to buy his archaeological find.

Rowland replied to the group's enthusiasm with great news. He was willing to sell them, and he had found many more pieces than he originally thought. Feeling how significant this find was going to be, he did state that they should all be part of one set and that he did not want to sell only part of the collection. He added that he would keep digging. Miss Babcock ponied up the sum of $500 to purchase his find. That's over $6,000 in today's money.

Soon, crates were being sent to Little Rock from Jonesboro, and checks were being sent from Little Rock to Jonesboro. The museum quickly spread the word of this historically significant find. It prepared the front window with the appropriate signage and made displays to hold the larger objects. It was going to be a great day for Arkansas when this exhibit opened.

Mr. Rowland now found the most impressive piece of the collection. It was a serious-looking head of a man with a heavy brow line, recessed copper eyes and inlaid brass earrings. The head was so regal that Babcock gave it the nickname King Crowley, supposing that this man must have been a king or leader of his people.

King Crowley made the centerpiece of the museum's front window display. News of the find and its ramifications for Arkansas's role in history made big waves. The newspapers covered the story and plastered King Crowley's picture across the front pages. The public turned out in droves to see the discovery and hear the story behind this event. An Arkansas professor was on site to validate the historicity of the exhibit. He confidently answered questions about the pieces and their meaning.

Rowland suggested that the artifacts were Egyptian or a lost civilization partially because hippos were unknown in this region of the United States. This is his hippo. *Photo by Heather Stanley.*

Such a sensation was the exhibit that a little over a year after its opening, men from the Smithsonian Institute wired ahead that they were coming and bringing a photographer from *Look* magazine. The arrival of these men in suits and the big media representatives made for big stories in the Arkansas press. Reporters covered the entire affair, from the airport to the museum to the greetings and introductions of the museum board and staff to the precise moment when the Smithsonian representatives did a collective "spit take" upon seeing the actual artifacts.

Contrary to the learned professor from Arkansas, the Smithsonian men were immediately of the mind that the objects were complete and utter fakes. A brief examination suggested to them that the pieces were no more than a year, or at the most two years, in actual age. They were not Aztec or Egyptian—they were junk. They were quickly identified as homemade in Arkansas. The only place they might ever hold in a museum would be as a doorstop or paperweight.

Bernie Babcock and her supporters now found themselves on the eve of a huge scandal, one that

A trio of Dentler Rowland originals once proudly displayed in the front window of Babcock's Little Rock Museum. *Photo by Heather Stanley.*

would make them and Arkansas look even worse than the criticism that had promoted the creation of the museum in the first place. Greatly distressed and hoping against hope that it was all a misunderstanding, Bernie sent desperate messages to Dentler Rowland about the validity of his relics.

In what can only be described as an exercise in unadulterated chutzpah, Mr. Rowland wrote back and said, "Them big men in the east don't know it all. They only want others to think they do. Anyway, they can say any thing they want to. It does not make it as they say." So there you have it. To Dentler Rowland, his word was as good as a trained archaeologist's. This is the Arkansas that H.L. Mencken spoke of.

Bernie still argued that the pieces were genuine for a time and finally relented and relisted them as genuine folk art by an Arkansas craftsman. But the damage was done. The credibility of the museum and its leaders was ruined. News of the fraud spread far and wide.

In the end, the collection was dispersed. A few choice chunks stayed in Little Rock, and thirty some odd pieces were eventually sent to the museum at Arkansas State University in Rowland's hometown of Jonesboro. The rest, including the head of King Crowley, was bought by an

Edward poses with one of the dopier looking items in the Rowland collection. *Photo by Heather Stanley.*

2 As every body thinks them big men in the east don't know it all. They only want others to think they do. Any way, they can say any thing they want to. It does not make it as they say. I will write later as to the book I wanted. I am very tired and must close hoping to hear from you soon.

so good by
from   dentler rowland
Oh yes, I will not sell any without selling all together they belong together and must stay together

This is the last communication from Rowland defending his collection. He took over $6,000 in today's money for the pieces he made in his shed. *Photo by Heather Stanley.*

anonymous collector from California. The mystery remains as to why this collector would want the fakes, let alone pay top dollar for them.

Some say there is a mystical quality to the Crowley head, and stories of strange phenomena associated with the head have circulated. Is there something more to this stone head than just a fake artifact? Does it have mysterious powers? Or has all this been planted by the collector to drive up interest in this once famous fraud? Well, all I can tell you is that it lives in a specially made museum box in my closet. After more than sixty-five years hidden from public viewing, I let the Crowley head out of the box once in awhile for an appropriate audience.

But what of H.L. Mencken and his war of caustic words upon Arkansas? The war escalated. The Museum of Discovery fiasco only provided fodder for his well-honed attacks. Having failed at stopping his argument about Arkansas's lack of culture, history and art, the state legislature voted on February 3, 1931, to pass a motion to pray for Mencken's soul to be saved. Once again, what Arkansas lacks in money, ability, knowledge and success it makes up for in religious zeal.

17

The Most Unnecessary Place on Earth

What follows is the strange but true story of Dogpatch, USA. It is the karmic crescendo to our journey into all things Bizarrkansas. This forgotten tale is absurd, funny and bittersweet all at the same time. It represents ambition; a thousand dreams from a thousand people; blood, sweat and tears; and, in the end, failure.

It all began in 1966, when a man named Albert Raney Jr. decided to put his family trout farm near Harrison, Arkansas, up for sale. Now if this were any other book, you might guess what would happen next: a man sells a trout farm in the Ozarks, people go fishing and the man selling the farm gets rich from the sale. Not a chance.

When Albert Raney Jr. listed his trout farm for sale, it triggered an idea in the mind of a man named Oscar J. Snow. Now, if this were any other book, you might not think that the name Oscar J. Snow was chock full of irony. But it is.

Mr. Snow gathered nine other men as investors and formed Recreation Enterprises, Inc. The ten men then approached satirist Al Capp with a crazy idea. They pitched the idea of buying up the trout farm and surrounding town of Marble Falls and turning it into a theme park based on Mr. Capp's *Li'l Abner* cartoon strip.

They showed him pictures of the area and described in great detail how the land and the people were a perfect fit to re-create the world of *Li'l Abner* in real life. And they convinced him that the time was perfect for such an endeavor.

If you dial your nostalgia vision to 1966, you will remember that all things rural were "in" at the moment. Television gave us *The Beverly Hillbillies*, *Green Acres* and *The Andy Griffith Show*. Likewise *Li'l Abner* and the country bumpkin residents in the cartoon town of Dogpatch were riding high on this wave of cultural comedy. In fact, *Li'l Abner* was doing so well that Al Capp had been approached by many corporations and individuals trying to capitalize on his success. He had always turned them down. That is, until now.

Miracle of miracles, Al Capp said yes to Oscar J. Snow and his partners. Recreational Enterprises, Inc., sprang into action, and the town of Marble Falls officially changed its name to Dogpatch, USA. Yes, the imaginary town of Dogpatch now existed in the real world. The only question remaining was whether the cartoon was going to become more real or if real life was going to get a lot more cartoony.

It made national news when staunch Bostonian Al Capp came to northwest Arkansas and spoke at the groundbreaking on October 3, 1967. The eight-hundred-acre park would sit within the one-thousand-acre land buy and offer the trout farm, a gift shop, horse-and-buggy rides, a train called the Pork Chop Spechul and, of course, performance art by the Dogpatch Players.

The Dogpatch Players were the actors and actresses who were recruited to portray the characters that Al Capp created in the *Li'l Abner* cartoon strip. Big, strapping young men played Abner, while curvy, robust young ladies took on the role of Daisy Mae. All the residents of Dogpatch were fleshed out in full costume, the buildings were the set pieces and the performances were nearly constant.

At any given time, you might be strolling along the streets of Dogpatch when characters would burst out on the scene

This is a vintage picture of Dogpatch's Pork Chop Speshul chugging along the tracks that ran through the once thriving theme park. *Photo courtesy of Charles Wetzler.*

and deliver the lines and action needed to re-create the Al Capp world. The directors of these performances were very strict about how each character was to be played, including a deep commitment to bad grammar. It was all consistent with the cartoon strip.

The first year of operation, Dogpatch reported an attendance of over 300,000 visitors at an admission of $1.50 each. The park was going to turn a profit in its first year. It looked like fortune was smiling on Dogpatch, something that was strangely out of sync with the cartoon world.

Al Capp's son, Colin, worked at the park that first season, where he met and married Vicki Cox, a young lady who was playing the part of Moonbeam McSwine. Happiness was everywhere in Dogpatch, USA. There was laughter, love and money.

Behind the scenes in 1968, a man named Jess Odom bought the controlling interest from Mr. Snow and some of the other investors who favored taking their profits and going home. Now holding the reins of Recreational Enterprises, Inc., some decisions were made to ensure that Dogpatch would draw an even broader audience from across the country and cement its place in theme park history.

These decisions included a long-term licensing agreement with Capp, the addition of campsites and other attractions to broaden the appeal of the park. Theme park rides were added, and in an effort to keep confidence in the park, former governor Orval Faubus was hired to be general manager. Yes, that Orval Faubus.

The next few years proved to be an increasing challenge to the business of the park but a golden era for those who came to love the park. This included many of the employees. This was especially true for those who served as entertainers. Many of them made lifelong friends during their time at Dogpatch. In fact, there is an annual reunion of cast members in the town of Harrison.

One cast member named Sally Riley Gotcher told me she played Daise Mae at Dogpatch back in 1975. In exchange for her daily labor, she received a grand total of $1.80 an hour with the promise of an additional $0.20 an hour if she stayed for the entire summer. Which she did.

While there may have been fun and friendship down in the park, up in the offices, trouble was brewing. Keeping up the park's profitability was proving to be a daunting task. Mr. Odom and Mr. Faubus had snugged up their thinking caps a little too tightly.

Two summers before Sally was singing and dancing as Daisy Mae, the company had bought additional land next to the park and had the next big attraction ready to open by Christmas: a ski resort.

Now, I know what you're thinking. You can't put a ski resort in northwest Arkansas. Ski resorts belong in places like Aspen, Colorado, not Harrison, Arkansas. There is a reason these things are true.

The Marble Falls resort opened and didn't do too badly at first. But the projected attendance figures prepared by a Los Angeles entertainment analysis firm were falling short in a major way. If this weren't bad enough for the inhabitants of Dogpatch, the decade of the 1970s held some devastating twists of fate that would spell doom for the inhabitants of Arkansas's only cartoon theme park.

Ironically, in Al Capp's musical and movie version of *Li'l Abner*, Dogpatch is considered "the most unnecessary place on the face of the earth." Dogpatch is targeted for destruction by powerful forces, including profits. One of the most famous songs from the show is "Progress Is the Root of All Evil." Oddly, it seemed the comic strip themes were catching up with its real-world parallel universe.

As the next years unraveled, the oil troubles in the Middle East drove gas prices up, the energy crisis came into full bloom, interest rates soared and a wave of cynical smarts ended the television era of rural and country comedy. If that weren't enough, the middle states of the nation faced a string of years with some of the warmest winters on record.

Marble Falls ski resort became a joke for comedians on late-night television as "Muddle Falls." And indeed, the warmest years on record made keeping the resort in snow impossible. Artificial snow machines churned out wet, sludgy, semi-frozen product in lieu of the white, fluffy product desired. The main activities available to vacationers staying at Marble Falls at that point included sloshing down the mud path and making a mud man with the kids or possibly a mud angel.

By the end of 1973, the company was $2 million in debt and was ready to borrow another $1.5 million in an unfriendly lending environment. In 1976, the banks began plans to foreclose on Dogpatch, USA. Jess Odom convinced his bloodthirsty note holders that Marble Falls was the problem. He closed the ski resort in an effort to stop the financial bleeding.

In 1977, Al Capp retired, and *Li'l Abner* vanished from America's funny papers overnight. Oddly, 1977 turned out to be one of the park's most profitable years since its initial opening season. But what followed next were a series of desperate tactics designed to keep Dogpatch afloat.

Odom let go of the Al Capp character licenses and tweaked the park into a generic hillbilly theme as opposed to *Li'l Abner* specific. Two personal injury lawsuits were filed against the park in 1979, as well. Odom attempted to convince the town of Harrison and its county counterparts to underwrite the park's debt with tourism bonds, but the plan was rejected.

And in what was arguably the worst yet most Arkansas option of all, Odom announced that he was negotiating to sell the park to another group of investors who wanted to transform it into a biblical theme park to be called the rather dyslexic name of "God's Patch." A massive heat wave in 1980 drove Dogpatch well below its operating expenses. In November, the park filed for bankruptcy.

The park changed hands and management a few times over the next few years, and thanks to fresh infusions of cash and many changes in staffing and presentation, it limped onward all the way to 1993. By the end, every possible promotional gimmick, corporate sponsorship and tie-in had been exhausted. Bits and pieces of the land were sold off or awarded as settlements in lawsuits. A couple businesses even managed to crop up around the fringe acreage of the park.

But the dream from the summer of 1968 was over. Perhaps the curse of the fictional Dogpatch came true in real life, or

Dogpatch, USA, faced the ravages of time and nature after its closing. There are still bits and pieces of the park and random memorabilia zealously guarded by fans and collectors. *Photo courtesy of Charles Wetzler.*

perhaps it was just a bad idea from the beginning. I would point out that just north of Dogpatch's now decaying carcass of old buildings, rotting statues and trampled memorabilia are Branson, Missouri, and Silver Dollar City. These tourist attractions managed to capitalize on rural life themes and culture but somehow grew into an American phenomenon.

Ironically, the original objection to the park by the Arkansas Department of Tourism had been that the theme of the park would only reinforce the long-standing, embarrassing Arkansas stereotypes of inept hillbillies. And now Arkansas has the strange but true story of the single most famous failed hillbilly cartoon strip–based theme park haunting its past. To all but those who lived the experience themselves, it has become a forgotten tale.

18

The Most Unfortunate Name

We began our journey through Bizarrkansas with my personal tale of encountering town names that seemed absurd and funny to my Yankee heritage. It is only fitting that we close with late-breaking news of the same.

In August 2012, a poll across seven English-speaking countries, taken by the genealogy website called findmypast. com, named Toad Suck, Arkansas, as having the most unfortunate town name in the entire United States.

References

Arkansas State University Museum
encyclopediaofarkansas.com
Museum of Discovery
Statehouse Museum
visitmyarkansas.com

About the Authors

Edward Underwood has been a museum curator, planetarium director, radio personality, theater producer, minister, ghost tour guide, magician and storyteller. He loves collecting  the forgotten tales of Arkansas and believes himself to be well on the way to becoming one. You can see what he is up to at www.remarkablearts.com.

Karen Underwood is an independent musician, singer and songwriter. She has written scores for major musical adaptations of famous literary works, including *Peter Pan* and *Alice in Wonderland*. She has toured and performed extensively and is currently innovating new musical fusion concepts. You can follow Karen at www.remarkablearts.com too.